T0281805

Y'ALL FIRED

Y'ALL FIRED

A SOUTHERN BELLE'S GUIDE TO RESTORING FEDERALISM AND DRAINING THE SWAMP

MANDY M. GUNASEKARA

FORMER CHIEF OF STAFF OF THE U.S. ENVIRONMENTAL PROTECTION AGENCY (EPA)

Since 1947
REGNERY
An Imprint of Skyhorse Publishing, Inc.

Visit our website at www.regnery.com.
Please follow our publisher Tony Lyons on Instagram @tonylyonsisuncertain.

10 9 8 7 6 5 4 3 2 1

Library of Congress Cataloging-in-Publication Data is available on file.

Cover design by Brian Peterson
Cover photograph by Rebekah Clayton Photography

Print ISBN: 978-1-5107-8260-0
eBook ISBN: 978-1-5107-8284-6

Printed in the United States of America

CONTENTS

DEEP STATE TARGET

Getting Back

Right now, it looks like President Trump will be returning to the White House in early 2025. President Trump's polling is strong, and his opponent is weak. Inflation remains high and confidence in the Biden government is plummeting on everything, especially in foreign affairs. Today, people can look at the Biden disaster and contrast it with President Trump's tenure. The choice is obvious, hence the positive polling for Donald Trump.

At the same time, Biden's absurd show trials of President Trump have boomeranged to the former president's benefit; no one is fooled as to what this Kafkaesque circus is about, which is scoring political points to distract from Biden's numerous failures. Biden believes that voters are so stupid that, if they see a picture of President Trump in handcuffs, they will forget all about how bad the last four years have been. This won't work.

As it stands, President Trump is getting back at his political enemies in the polls—all before entering office again. But at the same time, Biden and Co. are taking steps to get back at the former and future president, as well as his allies. Steven Bannon and Peter Navarro are two Trump allies and former officials who have been subjected to Democrat lawfare from the Biden government and its allies in Congress and elsewhere.

Any outspoken proponent of President Trump can become a target of the Deep State. Unfortunately, I am now among that number of Trump administration officials subject to legal harassment. In early May, my husband Surya was at our office in Oxford, in Mississippi, when two FBI officials and a representative from the Environmental Protection Agency's OIG (office of the inspector general) walked in. I just happened to be out of town at a conference in Oklahoma City.

The trio informed my husband that they were in town to serve me a subpoena related to an ongoing criminal investigation. Moreover, they told Surya that they were in the process of convening a grand jury.

Surya accepted the subpoena on my behalf without issue. The decision of the EPA OIG to wait until the metaphorical eleventh hour was a deliberate one. Because President Trump is poised to return to the White House next year, the partisans at EPA are taking preemptive steps to block me from returning in a leadership role.

This strategy is novel in that the Deep State wants to get at its opponents *before* they even enter into public service. As with Biden's lawfare against President Trump, the logic here is that, if partisans can sully my reputation with spurious charges, they can sink any potential confirmation vote or make the administration think twice before hiring me to a senior role.

Their additional goal is to create financial strain or even bankrupt me. Lawyers suited for addressing these types of subpoenas are not cheap and they know it. It's also why they punctuated the entire process with a veiled threat to my husband.

"You got any subpoenas for my time at CBP?" my husband asked as they exited our office (CBP, referring to his service at

U.S. Customs and Border Protection under the Department of Homeland Security).

"Not yet," said one of the agents.

And on that ominous tone, they left.

What We Are Up Against

Frustrating as this situation is, it is no surprise. In fact, it is totally on-brand for the Biden administration and its supporters in the civil service.

Throughout this book, I have discussed the plans and processes for reasserting control over the Executive Branch. All the while, I have noted that reform will be difficult largely because those in power do not want to give up their illegally seized influence and authority.

I will ultimately be fine, but I worry that many others will not be. This is all the more reason to see the reform effort for what it is: a risky, deeply rooted problem made all the worse by the activists seeking to reinforce the *status quo* at any cost, no matter how immoral or illegal.

I reject the Establishment Republican idea that we cannot reassert our rightful, constitutional authority over the federal government. But I do concede that it will be hard, and that there will be political casualties, i.e., those whose careers are harmed by a Deep State that takes issue with their service, even though they committed no misdeeds as political appointees.

To borrow a favorite word of President Trump's, D.C. is a truly "nasty" place. As conservatives, we will have few friends; and as reformers, we will have even fewer yet. We should be candid about this, but we should not be pessimistic. There is so much we can do, so much low-hanging fruit we can grab, that will go a long way in fixing things in our dysfunctional federal government.

To win these battles, we must keep in mind the important lessons explained, re-explained, and hammered home throughout this book, including the importance of planning, teamwork, loyalty, focus, and perhaps the most important, courage.

MISSISSIPPI MANDY

The Generational Challenge

As a military brat, I was raised with a deep sense of patriotism. Working for the government, whether military or civilian, was about service and duty. Needless to say, these were very happy points of reference, and they instilled in me a general optimism about America and an appreciation for its unique republican system.

And for years, those happy feelings were buttressed by a host of amazing events in my lifetime: the US winning the Cold War, the ascent of the American economy during the tech boom, and the resilience we showed in the face of the horrors of the 9/11 terrorist attacks, among many others. It was during this time that I developed a deep sense of patriotism, which in turn led me to pursue a career in public service.

Sadly, I would not have written this book today if I still felt as optimistic about and confident in the republic as I did years ago. Indeed, my personal experiences in and around government have shown me that politics in Washington, D.C. have become warped and harmful to the country as well as to our system of government. For the progressives who run the Deep State (i.e., the permanent government in D.C.), partisan goals have supplanted the Constitution as their proverbial North Star. This has led to the destruction of the all-important rule of law, and an attendant decline in trust in the government. This is neither desirable nor tenable; these degradations must be reversed.

I remain a positive person, but I am also a realist: we must change the *status quo* lest we risk losing our constitutional inheritance forever. In some respects, this is not a new phenomenon: there are always threats to liberty over time, and they rarely remain the same. To paraphrase President Reagan, our rights and liberties are always at risk, meaning each generation must do what it can to guard against domestic and foreign threats to our way of life. Since the fall of the Soviet Union, those threats have been primarily domestic, and that is still true today.

The salient difference today, however, is that the threats to our liberty are not individual problems, but comprehensive threats. For instance, consider how government agencies have chipped away at our privacy rights in the name of national security, as was the case during the presidencies of George W. Bush and Barack Obama.

Put bluntly, I'm talking about the challenges to how we conduct politics in this country, from the administration of elections to the making of rules and their enforcement (or lack thereof, as the case may be). This is the administrative threat that so many have warned against, and it's real. We must confront it.

It is my grave concern about those internal threats that led me to write this book. This is a book about American politics generally, and about the burgeoning crisis of legitimacy in Washington, D.C., in particular. Some commentators like to frame this problem as a nascent "Cold Civil War," which, while a great phrase, misses the nuance of the conflict. Without giving too much away on the front end, I see this problem as being more like a game dictated by certain rules than an existential battle of "all against all" governed by the Hobbesian idea of self-preservation above and before all else.

Similarly, I don't think a war metaphor is apt when only one side is fighting to consolidate power.

Politics in America were never meant to be existential—a truth underscored by the logic of and purposes served by our institutions, chief among them being the Constitution. Put differently, an election, a court ruling, an act of Congress—none of these things would, in the Founders' view and under their rules, change America in any fundamental way so as to put our existence as a republic at risk.

But I would be lying if I didn't admit that I do often worry that things are changing for the worse in my lifetime. Specifically, I see that political disputes *are* becoming more existential and, necessarily, less traditionally American. I find myself thinking about these threats all the time.

Political and legal norms that endured for centuries have been broken and forgotten in the last few years, with few in government or media giving these problems the coverage they deserve. At the same time, the membrane separating the political from the legal has been violated repeatedly, and it is difficult to imagine how it could be repaired at this point. But it could get worse, which is reason alone to try.

And these are but a few microcosms of the larger trends that continue unabated. From the endless and still ongoing persecution of former President Trump (now eight years running, which I believe makes him the most investigated person ever) to the weaponization of executive branch agencies to bludgeon everyday Americans into accepting ideas and practices they find unacceptable, the government in Washington has repeatedly done what was once unthinkable, and it does not appear deterred in the slightest.

As I see it, not only is our Constitutional order at stake (to the extent that key aspects of it are not already lost), but so is the entirety of the intangible political system of parity and understanding that informed and sustained our heretofore mostly healthy civic culture. If and when these barriers fully break apart, we will be faced with a series of problems so daunting and extensive that I worry we as a country will be irreversibly alienated from the Founders and their "more perfect" dream that they and generations of others sacrificed so much for to create and sustain.

And should the worst happen—should our constitutional republic be fundamentally transformed or thrown out—then I am confident in predicting that whatever government might replace it will be worse.

Consequently, preserving the political system we as citizens inherited is the most important task in our lives as Americans. I firmly believe this, but I am by no means the first to say it. So many great thinkers and leaders have touched on this idea in some way or another, and that's not because it sounds good (though it does), but rather because it is so integral to who we are as Americans. Without our unique system of government and the norms that make it possible, we would not be American citizens; we would simply be citizens like those in any other country. We would also be poorer, more susceptible to foreign threats, and overall, less successful. In my view, saving that system is absolutely essential.

Regrettably, many on the Left and Right do not understand this core truth, and thus likely do not agree with me on this point, let alone the contention that the federal government—the executive branch specifically—must be radically reformed.

For too long, Republicans in D.C. have tried to rationalize and normalize constitutional violations and the degradation of norms; in some cases, they have simply focused on other issues and declared them existential. And for just as long, Democrats and progressives across the federal government have violated the rules—written and unwritten—that define our system of government. This cannot be tolerated forever. This is a major theme of the book, and one I return to repeatedly.

In the following chapters, I explain and expand on my view of this dilemma—a perspective shaped by my own professional experiences, both during my time in the Trump Administration and after—before turning to the relevant history of how we arrived here. Along the way, I share some ideas on how to get out of this mess.

I firmly believe that a solution to this quagmire is both possible and pressing. In my view, this should be the singular focus of the next Republican administration. Thankfully, there are candidates running in the Republican Presidential Primary who understand this issue and are interested in rectifying it. In the final sections of the book, I review the plans and programs they have put forth.

But before getting into all the finer details, I think it's only right that I explain a bit more about who I am and why I see America as I do, and how I understand the current problems that ail her. To best give that context, I want to begin by sharing a short observation I made about American politics years ago.

Who I Am and How I Got Here

Something I noticed early in my political career is that people running for office and/or serving in office like to define themselves by their party. For instance, "I'm a liberal Democrat" or "I'm a Second Amendment Republican." There's nothing wrong with this, but for me, I have always seen the political labels as secondary. Put differently, these labels follow from the experiences that shape us.

Our decisions and views as citizens define who we are, not labels. This applies to so many of my fellow Americans, and to me and my family as well. Identity is based not on voting, but on one's upbringing; those formative experiences inform us as citizens because in the best cases they show us the importance of our relationships, both in our families and in the republic. And even so, to be clear, identity does not necessarily dictate politics. We are all individuals in this country, not members of groups—a point that my grandmother's life hammered home to me early on.

With that in mind, my own worldview was primarily influenced by my upbringing in Mississippi. And two people in particular made a huge impact on me: my grandmother Iris and my father, who served in the Air Force. I want to tell you a bit about them and how those relationships made me who I am.

Iris is, in my opinion, one of those once-in-a-generation people you meet who is far ahead of their time. Independent and with deep convictions and tenacity, Iris helped my grandfather to start and run his medical practice in Mississippi while raising three children.

And if that wasn't impressive enough, she was also a committed Republican activist in the Deep South when that was not easy to do. Democrats dominated everywhere, and Republicans were unpopular and even unwelcome. But she was undeterred. In fact, she was so firm in her convictions that she set up the Newton County Republican Party and helped establish engagement with the Mississippi Federation of Republican Women.

Her efforts didn't pay off right away. It took years for Republicans to gain a foothold and eventually to win elections. Mississippi is not red today because of her, but efforts like hers contributed to a massive political shift. In my view, that is an important reminder of what's possible when a person is sufficiently driven and loyal to their beliefs. The odds may be long at first, but nothing is set in stone; people and situations can change for the better.

I know that my earliest thoughts about being an active citizen stem from conversations with my grandmother, and I owe her a great deal for that. At the same time, I must mention my dad, because he is the other great influence in my life.

Dad worked as an active-duty air force officer, meaning we were constantly on the move depending on where he was stationed. This was a tough situation in some respects, but in others it was eye-opening. Not only did I get to meet all kinds of people, but I also got to see much of the world. I'll never forget our time in South Korea. It was there that I saw the Demilitarized Zone (DMZ), and it put in stark terms what freedom meant.

All of the moving we did helped me to understand how important family is, which is something I value tremendously. It also showed me what service meant in practice. My dad did whatever was asked of him by the military, often at great sacrifice and occasionally to the frustration of his family. If he had it his way, I'm sure we would have found a home in Mississippi and stayed there. But my dad's calling—to serve the United States—was bigger than that, so everything he did to advance that goal, he did so with a smile.

Seeing how diligently he worked, seeing that nothing phased him—these memories are seared into my brain, and I try to be the same type of person as Dad. One way I've tried to emulate him is through public service.

Serving has always been rewarding. After permanently moving back to the Mississippi, I loved to volunteer because it allowed me to step outside the town of Decatur where I spent the majority of my formative years. Small, rural, and with one stoplight, Decatur was not exactly a bustling city, so the opportunity to get involved—with local projects, organizations, etc.—was always a nice jolt of excitement in an otherwise sleepy town. Knowing that whatever work I did would help those around me was an awesome feeling, and it has stuck with me, even when I was hundreds of miles from home.

Most folks who grow up in Decatur never really leave. My path diverged when I won State in cross country my senior year. With a full-ride to the local community college, I hadn't really given much thought to attending a four-year college, until Mississippi College recruited me to run. Needless to say, this changed the trajectory of my life.

After graduating college, I went to law school because I understood that an advanced degree would allow me to do meaningful work to improve the country. Or, as I saw it, to serve in a more impactful way. This ended up being a great decision as it led me to the topic of regulation, which in turn allowed me to work in Washington, D.C. across the government, from Congress to the Environmental Protection Agency (EPA), to directly help those crushed by distant, onerous rules. Cutting red tape, returning money to taxpayers, and helping all Americans to secure the affordable energy they need to work and to live well are the most rewarding aspects of my work, and I love it.

The Bureaucratic Difference

My path to politics was not direct, and looking back, it's sometimes surreal thinking about how far from Decatur I am today. Working full-time while raising kids has been a challenge, especially as I've tried my best to impart to my kids these same Mississippi values that I was taught. It's been doubly tough when we're out of state, but the silver-lining is that this situation has forced me to think about my hometown, my people, and my values even more. The values we live by and the work we do mean a lot to our communities and to the formation of our characters, which is why I want my kids to be proud Mississippians like their ancestors and I.

Consequently, throughout my time in D.C., I have remained committed to the experiences, lessons, ideals, and people who shaped me in that small town. I always try my best to remember who I am—a proud, seventh-generation Mississippian—and those I serve, namely the taxpayers of all backgrounds, and the Constitution. Working with a smile and maintaining high character are two essential rules I hold myself to.

In Congress, this was easy to do. I worked as an attorney for the Republicans, and I was able to adhere to and promote those values in the workplace with little difficulty.

Sadly, as my role changed, it became more challenging to follow those self-imposed rules of conduct—honor, integrity, service—especially once I entered the progressive-dominated Executive Branch, which was openly hostile to those codes. What stood out to me about this was that, substantively, I was doing the same work. The only change was the branch, and thus the people I worked with, i.e., with bureaucrats rather than congressmen and their staff members.

One experience in particular during my time in the Trump Administration pushed me in ways I never could have anticipated. The silver lining (if it can be called that) was seeing the swamp up close and in a way I hadn't before. This misadventure opened my eyes to how rotten things really are, how underhanded the Deep State is, and how relentlessly it will work to frustrate all efforts at reform. Let's discuss the Paris Climate Accords and an ill-fated trip to Germany, because I think it perfectly captures the extent of this terrible problem.

CHAPTER I

WELCOME TO BONN

Deep State Target

I have spent a lot of time in Washington, D.C. In fact, much of my professional career has been spent on Capitol Hill. As an attorney, I know that so much of politics in the US is a process (passing laws, debating terms, etc.). As a conservative, I also know that these processes typically end up favoring Democrats and their more liberal positions—such is the nature of things in the post-Constitutional age of the Administrative State.

Frustrating as this situation is, it's one that most conservatives acknowledge and attempt to ameliorate, though the results are mixed. Holding hearings and threatening budgets are the typical *modus operandi* for congressional Republicans upset with an agency, and I was well-acquainted with this approach by the time I entered the Trump Administration.

What I didn't know until I served in the Executive Branch, however, is the extent to which entrenched interests—journalists, bureaucrats, and the broader Deep State—are willing to go *outside* of established processes to get their way. And stepping outside of the rules includes targeting and harassing political enemies, which is something I would have thought impossible only a few years earlier.

I openly admit that before President Trump's term in office, I would have laughed off any talk of a Deep State; I would have rolled my eyes at the suggestion that Democrats would employ extra-legal means to handicap their opponents. Sure, things like this happened in the past—under FDR and Johnson, for instance—but that was a *long* time ago. We live in a modern, first-world republic. Things like that don't happen here.

But after my experiences as an appointee, I'm sad to say that this is a real problem, and one that is only getting worse as polarization increases. And that is what this book is about—the problem with the permanent government, especially its willingness to disregard law, morality, and all norms to get its way. The following anecdote is just that: a story. But it is also a microcosm for the problem we as conservatives face in D.C., and one that highlights the intractable nature of the Administrative State. This in turn presents us with the all-important question: What must we do to change things?

One Moment in Time

I was blessed to serve the Trump Administration as a senior official at the Environmental Protection Agency (EPA) where I advanced POTUS's conservative agenda to the best of my ability. This position afforded me a unique perspective, and it was from this position that I observed the unyielding and pervasive effort on the part of the media and the Democrats in D.C. to create a new controversy each day over the course of the president's entire term. Their goal was to turn politics into a fever dream. This was true before President Trump took office, and it remains true today.

Crucially, it was also in this role that I began to take notice of other efforts—these ones, unlike those of the media, took place *within* government—that violated basic principles of our

Constitution. What I saw disturbed me: the political dynamics of the Executive Branch were warped and abused by conspicuously partisan bureaucrats. Over President Trump's four years in office, I saw that this issue was not local to one department; it was (and remains) a ubiquitous threat, including at the Department of Defense (DOD), an agency that virtually all Republicans in D.C. are deferential to, but which is financially irresponsible[1] and being pushed culturally Left.[2]

When I began to think about writing this book with the goal of informing everyday Americans about the problems with the unelected, permanent, bureaucratic government and explaining how to fix them, there was one anecdote that stood out in my mind, one series of events that remains vivid to this day.

This personal experience fully captures the threat of the Deep State and its unethical, often illegal opposition to government reform generally, and to President Trump in particular. What some may not know, and what I hope this story sheds light on, is that the permanent government is unprofessional, mean-spirited, and underhanded. These people are not experts, but they are politically aware, and they know that they are largely untouchable. As such, they can act as bureaucratic foot soldiers for the progressive cause without fear of punishment.

But before I can recount all the events in their entirety, we must first look back at an important promise that then-candidate Trump made to America, because it is where the story begins; that promise is central to the drama I experienced firsthand, which unfolded years later in Germany.

"We're Getting Out"

Even President Trump's most uncharitable critic must admit that, at a minimum, he is eminently quotable. I laugh whenever I hear some of his best lines from the 2016 Republican Primary, and I *really laugh* when I see the old videos of his debates with Secretary Clinton in the General Election. The man is constantly producing sound bites, sometimes unintentionally, and even out of office.

At the root of President Trump's speaking skills is the fact that he is a spectacular salesman and orator. I think his single greatest asset is his ability to brand things—people, ideas, and policies. In the 2016 Republican Primary, he famously defeated his rivals with his power to brand. He was equally effective at staking out his positions on policies. We all remember his comments on China and Mexico.[3] Equally important was his stance on American energy policy.

President Trump was an unabashed defender of America's incredible ability to produce affordable, safe energy. As a business-man, he understood that access to natural gas and other forms of energy that progressives hate is integral to the functioning of the American economy; these resources also ensure that Americans lead comfortable, independent lives. Unsurprisingly, recognizing this simple truth set him up against an increasingly radical environmental movement that, as of 2015 (and even more so today), had captured the Democratic Party.

As one can imagine, Democrats went ballistic when President Trump put on a miner's helmet and promised to protect and promote American energy and energy independence.[4] They lost all perspective on the energy issue. This reality is best demonstrated by Hillary Clinton's promise to put West Virginia coal miners out of work, because doing so is apparently necessary given the supposed threat of man-made climate change.[5]

Some progressives sincerely believe in this asserted threat, and they push policies that would slowly constrict the domestic energy sector, all while raising rates on hardworking Americans. Democrats can afford these price increases because their voters are either subsidized or so wealthy that rate increases won't affect them.

Because climate change is an "existential threat," the Obama Administration, as it so often did, sought to bypass the Constitution and its requirements to drastically reduce emissions—a move that necessarily would choke out local energy producers via the introduction of further, more onerous regulations.[6]

As we have seen, the Biden Administration is equally unhinged when it comes to energy policy; it has done everything imaginable to make the "Green New Deal" a reality while trying to convince Americans that a lower quality of life is fine.[7] And of course, it has tried to do so via Executive Branch regulations rather than through the Congress.

But before there was the Green New Deal, there was the Paris Climate Accords, or the Paris Agreement. The deal was an international agreement that would mandate sharp cuts in emissions by the US, as well as a substantial financial commitment to the Green Climate Fund; and it would do little to constrain the largest polluters, especially China.[8] Per usual, the Paris Agreement was mostly an act of moral grandstanding by the Europeans and American progressives—and one that the US taxpayer would feel the brunt of economically.

It should be said that the agreement is an obvious treaty given the obligations it would put on the US, so naturally the Obama

Administration avoided the Constitutional requirement that the treaty be ratified by declaring the deal an "executive agreement," i.e., something legally less than a treaty, but with all the appearances of a treaty. The upshot is that, under this standard, a future president could simply leave the deal since it lacked any binding commitment.

Candidate Trump promised to do just that, and his stance on the controversial agreement proved decisive in several Midwestern swing states during the 2016 Presidential Election.[9] Indeed, it was the Rust Belt—a region known for its manufacturing and energy-dependent economies—that came through and delivered one of the great upsets in American political history.

And yet, upon assuming the presidency, there was uncertainty as to whether President Trump would follow through on his promise to leave the agreement. Broadly speaking, there were two camps in the administration: those who wanted to get out, and those who, for various reasons, wanted to remain in the Paris Agreement.

My boss at the time, EPA Administrator Scott Pruitt, was firmly in the former group. He understood just how painful the Paris Agreement would be for ordinary, middle-class Americans, as well as those on the economic margins. In March of 2017, he was scheduled to attend a senior level meeting at the White House to discuss President Trump's course of action on the agreement. To say that there were serious stakes going into the meeting would be a massive understatement.

In my view, Administrator Pruitt was the perfect person to make the case for leaving the Paris Agreement: he was an attorney with an array of different experiences—a seasoned advocate and senior law enforcement official in the state of Oklahoma, to name two roles—that afforded him an incredible talent for distilling arguments and persuading others with the facts.

Similarly, as a former senior staffer in the Senate with a focus on the Paris Climate Agreement, I was the point person and attended nearly all of the official meetings prior to President Obama's signing of the so-called "executive agreement," an experience I recall well, as during the official trip to Paris I was eight months pregnant with my second child and had to get my doctor's written permission to fly there and back. I was well-positioned to brief Administrator Pruitt and to prepare him for what would be a highly contentious meeting, if not an open debate.

I understood the terms of the agreement, and Administrator Pruitt could make a bulletproof argument as to why we needed to get out. We were a strong duo, and I was convinced that, no matter what the other side argued, we would win.

As we prepared for the meeting, Administrator Pruitt told me that "we need to leave" and to not "let anyone change your mind"—no matter what the media would say or write. He reminded me that POTUS ran on leaving the unfair agreement, and that, at a minimum, exiting the deal would be symbolic to the climate agenda. He put it bluntly: leaving the agreement would be a clear signal to the world and to ideologues that America is proud of her successes, and that we embrace them and are unapologetic in doing so.

Armed with our "Paris Binder," Administrator Pruitt left the EPA and went over to the White House ready to spar with Director of the National Economic Council Gary Cohn, Secretary of State Rex Tillerson, and others who did not want to rock the proverbial boat by leaving a manifestly bad deal. I was anxious but confident in the administrator's ability to make his case.

We anticipated the likely arguments for staying, which went
something along the lines of this: The agreement, while imperfect
and certainly costly in some regards, would be good for business
because it would create new green jobs; and getting out would be
overly costly on a political level. This was the crux of the pro-Paris
argument in the White House.

Of course, this is only true if one believes in crony capitalism,
i.e., the subsidizing of companies and industries that, in an open
market, would fail on their own. The Solyndra Energy scandal
from the Obama years is a great example of the problem with this
approach: taxpayers fund bad business ventures that invariably fail,
and the money gets absorbed by connected political hacks.[10] And
this is to say nothing of the relative costs of the agreement; to write
off the costs as marginal is to ignore the rigor of a true cost-benefit
analysis, not to mention an assessment of where the costs would
be greatest., i.e., on the middle- and lower-classes.

As to whether a withdrawal would trigger bad press, well, that
struck us as irrelevant: this was Donald Trump's government we
were talking about—of course he was going to get bad press. Let
us not forget that the two scoops of ice cream he had for dessert
generated a hysterical panel at CNN and a bevy of articles on the
significance of his frozen treat.[11]

Finally, the efficacy of the agreement was dubious at best. Case
in point: China's "commitment" was conditional, noncommittal,
and vague.[12] China is a rising power, and one that has benefited
tremendously from American investments and favorable trading
terms. It is poised to become a true great power, and its leaders
understand that. The Chinese Communist Party (CCP) is playing
the long game, and President Xi's position *vis-á-vis* the agreement
was rooted in that logic. Basically, China would say nebulous

things about the agreement and progressives in the West would eat it up right now while Beijing would get the last laugh later when its competitors destroy their own economies.

The bottom line is this: If you do not have a real commitment from China on cutting emissions, then no amount of reductions by the US and the Europeans would move the metaphorical needle on climate change. As is typical, President Trump distilled this problem best: "China is ripping us off." This is as true of trade as it is for energy. For the US to be competitive, it cannot enter agreements that handicap its economy while China submits to no such limitations.

We walked into the Oval Office and sat in chairs directly across from the resolute desk flanked by the "let's just stay in" crowd. There is no better way to test the veracity of an argument than to be significantly outnumbered (which we were). Throughout the hour plus debate, the president was the quietest person in the room. Amidst heated debate he would ask simple questions. Why should we stay? Should we get out? "Yes, sir. We should get out," I emphasized numerous times. Ultimately it came down to one question President Trump constantly returned to: "But what will this do to the American worker?"

This point resonated with President Trump, and it proved decisive. I was thrilled to learn that Administrator Pruitt's arguments won the debate at the White House. Even more exciting was the news that President Trump wanted us to write the press release for the US withdrawal. The idea was to discuss a new path, one led by America, that would pivot from "Paris to Pittsburgh" and which would promote best practices, redirecting funds and the balancing of environmental imperatives with economic realities.

We quickly got to work on the press release. We were ready with a statement, but were ordered to stand by. Over the next few months, we were a part of numerous meetings, some planned and some spur of the moment.

This time period was an absolute rollercoaster of hard work, emotional ups and downs, and deep uncertainty. For two months nothing happened, and we began to worry that our opponents in the White House had somehow defeated us by stalling (a common tactic in D.C.). And then, finally, we were told to prepare for a Rose Garden event where the POTUS was to deliver a speech.

We were honored and thrilled to attend the historic event wherein the president announced "we're getting out" or renegotiating. In standard Trumpian fashion, he took action while leaving the door open for more talks and the establishment of a better alternative. Soon thereafter, we were informed that there would be new discussions, and I learned that I would have the opportunity to participate as a member of the official US delegation.

Originally set to be hosted by Fiji but moved to Bonn, Germany due to logistical limitations, I switched gears to begin preparations for what would be a momentous conference on the future of American involvement in global/energy talks. Little did I know, the trip would be much more than that; in fact, it would prove to be a nightmare—albeit a clarifying one.

The Untouchables

As I looked ahead to the fast-approaching conference in Germany, I began to coordinate with my counterparts at the State Department. Being part of the US Delegation was an honor in its own right; but including EPA in the larger planning and organization of the trip was something else entirely. As was often the case with the Trump presidency, this was not how things were typically done. The standard practice was to delegate to the experts at the State Department. The president knew that was no option for advancing his concerns, so he tapped us to represent his position abroad.

I quickly realized that those I would need to cooperate with at the State Department were less than thrilled about this arrangement. In a Democratic administration (and certainly in ordinary Republican governments, too), it would be the foreign policy "experts"—not EPA appointees—who would make plans for such a consequential meeting. (Never mind that deferential treatment of these supposed experts has never advanced the conservative cause generally—and that is to say nothing of the particular sphere of foreign policy.) And this is especially true when it comes to questions of climate change and energy.

But for POTUS, the entire focus needed to be different: he wanted stakeholders and those with an understanding of the energy sector and environmental concerns involved—in other words, the actual stakeholders and experts. In my view, this is reflected in his emphasis on what these costly policies would mean for working Americans; as with his questioning during the debate at the resolute desk, he wanted to be sure that the result of the policies in question would help America and her people more than it would undermine them.

The upshot is that the American approach to this conference would represent a massive shakeup and a change from the norm, so we anticipated some pushback. What we encountered was a full-on shove.

Upon entering the State Department's headquarters in Foggy Bottom for those first planning meetings, I sensed the sharp resentment of the career employees. I remember the feeling of dozens of eyes glaring at me. If you have ever been the subject of some melodrama in middle school and stepped into the auditorium or cafeteria before a group of hostile peers, then you can understand exactly how I felt. And this is a fitting analogy as many State Department employees behaved like middle schoolers in their interactions with us. (There was lots of pouting and whining, to put it kindly.)

Our discussions (or attempted discussions) with the State members of the delegation were marked by recalcitrant antipathy. No one wanted to share information with us concerning the strategy, and all of our efforts for clarification were burdened by a slow, painful, and too often fruitless process. This was my first encounter with an enduring problem when attempting to coordinate with partisan bureaucrats: the willful withholding of information. We were never given the whole story on what we were doing, and unless we asked perfectly crafted questions, we had no chance of getting all the necessary information.

And all of this is separate from the overt politics we encountered in these meetings. One particularly combative and subversive employee gave us such a hard time that we decided to look her up to find out what her issue was. As it turns out, we easily found a link to her Facebook page and saw that she had recently attended the Dakota Access Pipeline (DAPL) protest out West.

Was it any surprise that she and others like her wanted to isolate us? The policies we were tasked with carrying out were wholly unacceptable to them, and they were fully prepared to make life miserable for us by hamstringing our efforts to advance those policy goals.

This situation was emblematic of the larger issue *vis-à-vis* appointee-career interactions, namely that ideological bureaucrats were willing to manipulate their institutional knowledge and control of processes to retard the efforts of the political appointees tasked with advancing the agenda of the winning candidate. This is a total subversion of the American democratic system, and it is unacceptable. Unfortunately, we had no recourse. Our only choice was to try to push ahead.

Under the Constitution, those with opposition to President Trump and his conservative agenda only have two options under the law: continue in their roles and implement his programs, or resign. Many State Department officials opted for the latter, which is commendable. But many who stayed decided instead to act as guerrillas and sabotage the president's agenda. I repeat: this is illegal and antithetical to our system of government.

Returning to the delegation, the time eventually arrived for us to organize our travel plans. For those who do not know, traveling as a government employee is not as simple as it is for the president; there is no Air Force One to whisk you away to a meeting out of town. In fact, traveling as a government employee is a huge ordeal; there are all manner of logistics to figure out, from booking hotels to setting up an accurate itinerary for transparency and reimbursement purposes.

Consequently, we did what everyone in our situation does: we deferred to the full-time employees whose job it was to arrange our travel, especially for the international trip where the US-based EPA logistics team will often coordinate with an on-the-ground US embassy team that has insight on local accommodations. We trusted that everything would be set up without a hitch.

As the day of the trip approached, we (myself and a Deputy for Policy, another young professional woman) were informed that, due to space constraints, the scheduler was forced to get us a hotel outside of Bonn. Rather than everyone staying together, the delegation would be broken up at different hotels. The conference would be a huge event, so that made sense to us. We are low-maintenance and we were focused on the trip, so we didn't dwell on it.

It was not until we arrived in Bonn and boarded a taxi to our hotel that we realized something was amiss. We drove for miles outside of the city; with each passing minute, we moved farther away from our destination. Finally, after a 45-minute ride the wrong way and then another hour-plus in the right direction, we reached our destination. The hotel was not the nicest to look at, which was fine. After all, government employees do not need to use taxpayer money to stay at swanky resorts, especially when conducting official business.

We entered and were surprised by the vibe of the place; for a small European hotel, it was not particularly welcoming. We tried to ignore the fact that the atmosphere was off and decided to focus on getting food and settling in. Much to our chagrin, we were informed by the receptionist that we would need to wait several hours for the only local restaurant to open. The receptionist also clarified the one-pillow policy (one per bed), which made no sense to us, but we said that was fine. Because we spent our remaining cash on the marathon taxi ride and there was no ATM on site or close by, we had limited options. At that time, use of credit cards was hit or miss. We would need to wait around. So, we decided to get comfortable in the meantime.

Frustrated and fatigued from the trip itself and the lack of food options, we went to our rooms determined to relax for a few hours before dinner. Though we could not describe it just then, we both knew something was wrong.

We put our bags down and began to scan our surroundings. The room was a bit dark and there was indeed only one pillow per bed. Beyond that, there was a notable amount of adult-oriented paraphernalia. The more we looked, the more we saw.

Maybe it was the menagerie of sex-related items, perhaps it was the designation of the room as a "FKK Zone—nudists only" which was plastered on the interior door to the bathroom. Whatever it was, we finally figured out what was going on: we were staying in a German sex hotel.

As much as we were shocked and offended, we felt more grossed out than anything else. A foreign sex hotel is a disgusting place, and likely an unsafe one given the types of people who frequent these establishments. It was not surprising that a State Department employee would do something nasty to two young conservative women (though it was pretty ballsy, given that we were still in the midst of the pre-Biden[13] #MeToo moment), but it was shocking that someone would do something like this to two members of the American delegation on such an important trip.

This was an unmistakable message: we do not respect you, we do not recognize your right to be here, and we are going to make your job hell. And hell it was. We immediately began to phone our coworkers back in the US to try to rectify the situation. My Chief of Staff called the State Department, which acted incredulous about the entire ordeal.

After a substantial wait, we received a call from a State Department employee who jokingly said that he "heard you have issues with your hotel, right?" The call was highly condescending and, in the end, a waste of time. Later on, the agency took the problem seriously (or semi-seriously) when it realized how bad our ordeal was. Unfortunately, we were informed that, regrettably, there were no hotels available for us, and no taxis on their way back to Bonn for another 90 minutes. In all likelihood, then, we would need to stay the night.

That was unacceptable. As we were asking the hotel to call for a taxi, which was a minimum 90-minute wait, we saw a taxi—or at least a car that looked like a taxi—pull up to the front of the hotel. Perhaps our luck was starting to change, and we could snag this taxi before it left.

I ran outside and flagged down the driver with the goal of negotiating the price and an agreement that we would need to stop by an ATM somewhere in Bonn. As I approached the car, the driver greeted us with a menacing glare. He stepped out of the car and turned it off. He then lit a cigarette and blew smoke in my face. I stood there dumbfounded, but walked back into the lobby to wait for the next taxi. Perhaps fifteen minutes later, two women entered his car and drove off. In retrospect, it was better that we did not get a lift from a pimp.

Depressed, we finally accepted that we were likely stuck in the sex hotel for the night. That is no exaggeration: the US State Department hemmed us in with pimps and prostitutes in a German sex hotel.

The following day after we had arrived at the conference, back in Bonn, we were finally able to convince a State Department liaison to take us seriously. Over dinner, we told him about what was going on and he seemed to find it humorous, but indulged us nonetheless and agreed to go to the hotel with us to check it out. When he came out of the hotel, his tone was changed. He realized exactly what was going on, and how unfunny it really was. He saw the purple lights and openly displayed sex paraphernalia and was, like us, mortified. Yet, due to the late time of day coupled with his inability to make any logistical decisions without sign-off and assistance from the official logistical team, he still was unable to move us out of the location.

That night, I couldn't sleep and decided to do my own research and found an open hostel closer to Bonn. The State Department was still uncooperative and/or ineffective, so I decided to break protocol by reserving a room for us with my own funds. I did not make this decision lightly, as I knew it would entail a huge controversy and runaround to get reimbursement. But I refused to spend another night in a sex hotel. I had no other option.

The next day we made the move over, but the damage was done. We were seriously rattled by the experience and decided to return to the US early. What was to be the highpoint of our careers at that time was instead a sickening disaster, and one I could not forget about fast enough. Determined to not let these people win, we meticulously documented what had happened: we made notes, took pictures, saved emails, etc. In the end, we shared all of this with the State Department and were at least somewhat optimistic that it would result in disciplinary action for those responsible.

But, with Secretary Tillerson at the helm, careers more or less ran the department, and nothing came of our formal and well-documented complaint. Indeed, all that really happened was that: 1) the person or people who made our travel arrangements had a good laugh; and 2) he/she succeeded in undermining the mission of the delegation.

For the unassuming tourist, landing a reservation at the sex hotel may be an honest oversight, especially today. The website and reviews have seemingly been cleaned up since 2017. But a part of an embassy's purpose in a local community is learning the ins and outs of culture. Understanding the true experience at an infamous hotel would be common knowledge among our nation's foreign affairs specialists. Coupling this with condescending reactions in real time and the reality that I, and my fellow EPA politico, were the only two at the location makes it hard to swallow as a simple oversight; rather, it was an obvious act of bureaucratic bullying.

Lessons Learned

The entire ordeal was a disaster for us personally. It was humiliating and remains the rudest thing anyone has ever done to me.

Unfortunately, this incident was not isolated and there are numerous examples of how the Deep State regularly delivered its message that we Trump appointees were not welcome and sought to make our lives a living hell.

But I am a positive person; I am always on the lookout for silver linings, because if you do not seek them out, life can be very bleak. And in our case, this was the lone positive we took away from the experience: When you are a progressive bureaucrat, government institutions let you do almost anything to Republican political appointees.

From violating the spirit of the then-ascendant #MeToo movement to engaging in behavior that would in any other industry result in firing and a permanent and well-deserved professional blackballing, bureaucrats can do what they like. They are unaccountable and untouchable, and they understand that in a way that most Republicans do not. They are the permanent bureaucracy. President Trump took a lot of heat for it, and perhaps did not always articulate his position consistently, but this is the Deep

State (or Administrative State) he derided: a coterie of protected, partisan, rent-seekers who do not work for the president unless he is a Democrat, in which case they are full steam ahead. When a Republican occupies the White House, they are constantly pumping the brakes.

To reiterate, the federal bureaucracy is unlike many other institutions in America in that there is zero accountability. A lot of people on both sides of the ideological aisle like to talk about how "D.C. is broken," when in fact this is not true in the way they mean it. Rather, D.C. functions perfectly well for progressives—a point I hope to make in the following sections of the book by tracing more distant political history to the politics of our age; to the extent it doesn't work for them, it's a function of the fact that there is a majority of Republicans somewhere in Congress or on the Supreme Court. For Republicans, however, the bureaucracy is indeed broken, and it cannot be fixed.

But I also want to emphasize the importance of looking ahead, because this novel problem in our government—this extra-constitutional fifth column—requires new solutions because it is not a part of the original constitutional system.

Far too many Republicans, and even a significant number of conservative activists (i.e., those people who hold traditional views on the Constitution first and identify as Republican voters/party-members second), fixate on the ideal of civic reform, of returning to tradition, as a cure-all to our political maladies. If we simply return to the American political language of rights and responsibilities, engage in the political process, and allow our institutions to flourish, the argument goes, everything will be fine, e.g., politics will deescalate and people will develop realistic and originalist understandings of the government and their relationship to it.

There may have once been truth to this theory, but in practice, our institutions are rotten to the core, and have been for decades. For at least the last century, progressives have succeeded in commandeering and transforming the institutions of American government, and in turn people's expectations for them.

The twisted laws, practices, and politics of today would be unrecognizable to Americans of recent generations, and that is to say nothing of those who designed our political system. What would James Madison think when looking at an "independent agency" with the power to make and enforce its own laws? The crucial lesson I learned from my experience in Bonn was this: our Constitution is violated to such a degree that it is effectively a non-factor in shaping and refining the political attitudes and practices of bureaucrats and other partisan actors.

Understanding that this perversion of our government was intentional and successful is the necessary first step in making the sorely needed and decisive changes to restore the original Constitution and the system it established. The way I see it, this is the essence of President Trump's call to "drain the swamp." D.C. is a dark, stinky, difficult-to-navigate bog, and the genesis of so much of that filth is a bureaucracy borne from a competing Constitution, one that only came into being in the twentieth century.

As such, destroying the institutions of the rival constitution is absolutely essential if we are serious about restoring the original Constitution; these two imperatives are tied at the hip. Anything short of that is hollow rhetoric—something Republicans get enough of from their bad representatives on the campaign trail.

To be clear, this is a momentous challenge, and one that will require many different reforms, diligent work from thousands if not millions of activists, and a commitment to the long game.

Nonetheless, there is work we can do now, plans we can organize around and perfect, that will go a long way in addressing this existential problem. This book, *Y'all Fired: A Southern Belle's Guide to Restoring Federalism and Draining the Swamp*, captures one major goal of these plans. As the title suggests, it entails returning the original Constitution to its place at the center of the American political universe, which necessarily requires the termination of the usurper constitution(s) of FDR and LBJ. It is only through this process that we can drain the swamp.

If the Administrative State is a monster, then it is a hydra from Greek mythology: a snake-like reptile with many heads and the capacity to regenerate itself; when one head is severed, two grow back. To kill such a beast is no easy task. As the legend goes, Hercules succeeded only because he had a plan and help from allies who stuck to that framework. If we are to succeed in our endeavor of restoring the government to its constitutional limits, then we too need a plan. And like Hercules, we can only craft a successful plan if we understand the anatomy of the monster.

With that in mind, much of this book looks at the swamp itself. And that, in turn, requires an examination of the Administrative State and its origins. In the next section, I recount the relevant political history of how we ended up in this mess.

CHAPTER 2

THE SWAMP IS REAL

You've Been Deep Stated—Now What?

The Bonn fiasco was awful, and I wish it had never happened. But it did happen, and as I mentioned, it was a clarifying experience: it showed me how bad things really were in an administrative agency, and how far away we were from addressing the root problems in our government, namely the lack of accountability and the anti-democratic ethos of the bureaucracy. The bureaucratic harassment in Bonn reaffirmed my belief in the importance of public service. I was even more determined to fix this mess, to hold people accountable, and to advance President Trump's agenda.

I want to make explicit a point I alluded to in the introduction: the sexually-tinged hazing—gross and unacceptable as it was—was really the secondary issue. The bigger problem was that bureaucrats, in going out of their way to mistreat us, were really trying to undermine the president and the agenda he was elected to enact. This is a violation of the most basic premise behind our republican system established by the Constitution, which is that the people rule.[14] And that goes for the Executive Branch, too; the American people own it and set its direction when they select the president.

If you take the Constitution seriously and believe that it is central to our legal and political systems, then this was an act of illegal sabotage by a partisan cabal that is supposed to serve the people generally, and President Trump in particular. The voters pick representatives who direct the state toward their interests. The only role bureaucrats have in this process is assisting the Executive Branch—*led by the president*—in that goal. Anything else is forbidden.

Seeing the open disregard so many bureaucrats had for the law was infuriating. We knew that they deliberately wronged us to hurt President Trump. We also knew the law was on our side. So, we followed the complaint processes to the best of our abilities and sought justice for the awful situation they put us in over in Germany. Nothing came of it.

From this point forward, I no longer had any illusions about the task before us as conservatives working in the Executive Branch. This was the other aspect of the lesson we learned from Bonn: as conservatives, you're mostly on your own when dealing with the Executive Branch's bureaucrats.

To be clear, I was not oblivious to the context of serving President Trump as an official in Washington, D.C. Things were obviously going to be tough. I knew that we were in a Democratic city influenced by a liberal culture, and that we sought to enact change within thoroughly progressive institutions. What I never imagined was the degree to which we were powerless in the face of this challenge.

In my mind, I assumed that while law and political norms would constrain and shape our policy goals and strategies as appointees, they would apply equally to the bureaucrats with which we would compete against and work beside over the course of President Trump's tenure. Some true public servants exist, and I was fortunate to work alongside them. But they are the exception. Many bureaucrats are partisans; many others are there to collect a paycheck and are simply unhelpful. In both cases, I realized the hard way that many in the bureaucracy exist outside the law. Unsurprisingly, they have little regard for norms and the reputations of the institutions they work in.

The Deep State, the permanent bureaucracy, the Administrative State—whatever you want to call it—was not just a rhetorical flourish by President Trump. Rather, it is a concrete entity that exists, and it is thoroughly opposed to any attempts at reform and restructuring. It is a powerful force that is insulated from the vicissitudes of politics, and it will do whatever it can to undermine the state from being used for anything but progressive ends. It has its own rules and logic.

But do not expect it to police its own behavior. As David Bernhardt incisively and repeatedly points out in his book on the Administrative State, *You Report to Me: Accountability for the Failing Administrative State* (2023), failure is everywhere and accountability is nowhere in the Executive Branch.[15] Firing bad employees, reforming ossified processes and departments, addressing time-sensitive challenges—these basic tasks any serious, sizable organization faces are impossibilities for the permanent state.

What David gets wrong, however, is his assertion that the Administrative State is failing. From my view, it looks as strong as ever. Consider that in the last few years, it has succeeded in being openly partisan—even to the point of breaking the law—all while maintaining unanimous support from Democrats; at the same time, it has received, at best, empty criticism from Republicans in Congress. In fact, budgets for the most egregious defenders (e.g., the FBI, CIA, DOD, and IRS) have grown, including under the rule of Republicans.[16]

Still, there is some truth to David's contention. These agencies have demonstrated an incredible capacity to fail at instituting basic reforms and struggle to complete menial tasks, such as audits.[17] The reason for this sustained failure is that this entity is ultimately a satellite outside of the constellation of institutions and actors established under the Constitution. To the extent it can *really* be controlled is largely via funding and rule-making, which falls in part on Congress. But as noted above, congressional Republicans have, for various reasons, little interest in exercising their powers in a meaningful way on this topic—a problem that may be influenced by their financial portfolios.[18]

The upshot, then, is that federal elections mean very little when it comes to the direction of the government in Washington. But the problem remains, even if it isn't being addressed.

A Foreign Threat

To see why we were denied justice, and why one should assume that any future Republican president and his or her appointees will grapple hopelessly with the same cyclical struggles, one must look back at the relevant history, all of which occurred well after the close of the eighteenth century, when the Constitution was written and took effect.

I think the natural starting point is with the bureaucracy. This foreign body—the Administrative State—does not fit neatly into our political system for an important reason: it is alien to and thus incompatible with the Constitution.

The main reason for this incompatibility is found in the fact that the permanent state transcends multiple political categories that are otherwise entirely sequestered, e.g., rule-making powers are *meant* to be local to the Legislative Branch, Executive Branch officials are *supposed* to work for the president, etc.[19]

Today, for example, agencies at least partially (but not wholly) under the umbrella of the Executive Branch can make and judge their own rules, which is a conspicuous violation of the all-important principle of the Separation of Powers. While courts are finally taking issue with this illegal practice, they are a long, long way away from righting the proverbial ship.[20]

Indeed, under the Constitution, the powers allocated to the three branches are limited to *those branches* and must remain so. The system of competition between branches to keep the others in compliance breaks down quickly once this essential rule is violated, thus the emphasis by the Founders on creating a government in which the branches (and the people who populate them) are legally separated from each other, and indeed are incentivized to aggressively protect their particular powers. While there could of course be moments of healthy cooperation, they imagined the norm to be one of self-interested and vigorous competition.[21]

Sadly, this tenet was fatally undermined long ago, and we live with the consequences of that tragedy today. The cumulative effect of these violations led to the degradation of political norms and behaviors, and in turn established a new political culture and attitude, as well as a new legal regime. In my opinion, "the swamp" that President Trump discussed on the campaign trail and in office is an amalgam of those constitutional violations; it is a Frankenstein testament to the mistakes older generations made in turning away from the Constitution and its requirements.

Cumulatively, those gradual violations ushered in the arrival of a new political era with its own processes and norms. In my view, this epoch came about in the New Deal period, though its usurper constitution was only possible through important changes decades earlier. The most obvious legacy of this constitutional revolution is the ubiquitous call by progressives to "trust the experts" within the bureaucracy; it replaced the wisdom of deferring to the constitutional tradition and its rules and norms. In only a few generations, the form of American self-government set out by the Constitution was lost.

All of this is to say that President Trump's call to "drain the swamp" is a much more daunting and important task than many realize. One reason why this will be such a monumental challenge is the fact that the swamp has accumulated layers of sediment below its murky waters—and these layers of dirt have congealed into a thick mud over the decades. Understanding the layers individually and in relation to each other is the only way to grasp the scope of the swamp's rot, and in turn, to begin the arduous task of draining it. We need to look at the unconstitutional origins of the morass to understand how to dredge it.

The Money Train to Washington

I think that the truly unique feature of our Constitution as a charter for government is its deference to and elevation of local rule. (The Founding generation felt very strongly about this, which makes sense given that this is what the Revolution was all about). It is no coincidence that the document is arranged in such a way that the limits on government action apply largely at the federal level; the corollary is that much was left open to the states, including following or ignoring the federal Bill of Rights, at least for a time.

Thus, the integral aspect of the Constitution is that it makes states potent entities with which the federal government must negotiate and contend when it tries to take nationwide actions. When the Constitution and its terms are taken seriously, it is plain that the document gives states significant leeway and the capacity to officiate their own affairs. Indeed, the presumption cuts in their favor. For most of American history, powers that the federal government is known for today, such as raising taxes, were largely (and often exclusively) in the proverbial hands of various states.

I think this is a good segue into a discussion on the beginnings of the swamp, which is the erosion of federalism. Federalism, or the division of political powers between two competing powers (state governments and the government in Washington, D.C.), creates a very deliberative, slow-moving, and moderate political situation due to the fact that it necessarily splits up political power across entities—a reality that inherently pumps the brakes on radical change and popular sentiment.

Since the early 1800s, the US has moved further away from the federalist foundations of the country. Some of this movement has been expected and uncontroversial, i.e., the maturation of the US as a country necessitated greater federal authority in some areas of the economy. As such, I think that we can track the death of federalism to the early twentieth century, as most of the changes to federalism to that point were needed and natural; the corollary is that what followed was unnecessary, unnatural, and unhelpful.

Lots of conservatives point to the figureheads of the Progressive Era—Presidents Wilson and Roosevelt, or Justices Brandeis and Frankfurter—as the drivers of the left turn in American politics. While this is partially true, I think it is more valuable to look at the events that kicked off the rise of progressivism, as these events made the transformations of the early 1900s possible. And that means looking briefly at the movements and years that came before its mainstream ascent.

In the late 1800s, labor movements were on the rise. Socialist parties were big in Europe decades earlier (this makes sense as these societies industrialized more rapidly and generally had less social mobility, which creates frustration and class envy) and their ideas eventually made their way to North America,[22] including the United States.[23] Then, as now, these outright socialist and quasi-socialist populist parties advocated for government intervention in markets; they also pushed for certain benefits for their supporters. The salient difference back then, however, was that the government was far more constrained in redistributing wealth for the simple reason that it lacked the ability to collect money in the first place.

It may sound amazing given how much money Washington collects, redistributes, and wastes today, but back in the 1800s and in the first decade of the 1900s, the vast majority of federal money was raised from tariffs (some came from excise taxes, but not much).[24] This is because there was no income tax; the only one that had been implemented was a relic of the Civil War, which relapsed shortly after its conclusion.[25]

What is more, these activists were unhappy with the *status quo* because, they contended, tariffs ultimately hurt the working classes that they purported to represent. As a result, they wanted a new means for collecting money to redistribute. They ultimately pushed hard for income taxes so as to take money only from those individuals who they believed could afford it. Advocates seemed to get their way with the passage of the Wilson–Gorman Tariff Act in 1894, but it was summarily struck down by the US Supreme Court in *Pollock v. Farmers' Loan & Trust Co.* on the grounds that income taxes are a form of direct taxes, and thus can only be legally instituted at the state level.[26]

Article I, Section VIII of the Constitution is referred to as the "Taxing Clause" because it mandates that direct taxes be allocated on the basis of population, which translates into a system whereby state liability is dictated by population.[27] Hypothetically, if Virginia had fifteen percent of people out of the total population as of 1885, then under a direct tax, it would pay fifteen percent of the tax. This was a powerful check on direct tax regimes because it made their implementation far more difficult for those who wished to institute them to advance their partisan, redistributive ends.

Incensed and determined, activists began to look for a way around the Constitution. They settled on an amendment to the document, which they pushed for starting in the early 1900s. The Sixteenth Amendment eventually passed, and the Revenue Act of 1913—i.e., the now permissible but still unwise federal income tax—followed shortly thereafter. Progressives now had a means of funding federal initiatives. Money, and necessarily power, was slowly shifting towards Washington, D.C., and in the American zero-sum political system, this meant that states were losing influence. This has continued over time, meaning that greater cash flow to Washington translates to more power leaving the states.

When more money went to Washington, two things happened. First, this led to the creation of a cottage industry around the D.C. region to manage the money and its allocation. If there is more money in the federal government, then there will be a heightened need for employees to track and spend it. This led to growth in the government workforce, and the secondary and tertiary effects of this development caused other population and economic growth in the bordering areas.

Second, and more politically, the increase in money into the federal government increased its size, which created a novel situation: the government became bigger, and in turn more convoluted and labyrinthian. In the coming years, more departments started up, the government took on new responsibilities, money became harder to track, whole industries sprung up around the state, etc.

Ultimately, the federal government's processes became more obscure, its interactions with other entities more common, and all the while its size and scope changed in numerous ways. This transformation created a new demand, namely for government expertise. This applied to states, and later industries and even groups of people with shared interests and goals. A new class of people was thus needed to run and navigate the new government. At the same time, this led to the rise of lobbyists and attorneys who would advocate for clients to those administrators.

Money is a powerful force. Just as it can change people, it can change institutions, too. That is exactly what happened to the federal government. Once the spigots turned on, Washington grew to ever larger sizes, and in only a short period, its influence dwarfed those of the once powerful states on its borders and throughout the country.

Democratic Degradation

Turning to the other large transformation that killed federalism in the pre-Progressive Era, I think it is again important to look at the Seventeenth Amendment. For those who do not know, this amendment to the Constitution changed a subtle but important aspect of the original Constitution, namely the way in which senators were selected.

In the years prior to the passage of the Seventeenth Amendment in 1913, the Senate was one of the finest and most practical aspects of the little-r republican approach to the problem of democracy. That is, voters are often irrational, bad at long-term planning, and easily manipulated, so the Senate was a good buffer against those problems.

This is because the Senate's intelligent design allowed it to function independently of moral panics and other foolishness from the public, and it did so to a high degree. And how did this work? Basically, the elites in the various states would select enlightened statemen from among their ranks who would be appointed to serve. The Founders understood that a democracy is a bad thing without the proper guardrails limiting the tyrannical whims of the majority; they saw that putting too much decision-making power in the hands of ordinary people has diminishing returns.

Thus, to protect against the authoritarian instincts of mobs, they created a quasi-aristocratic class of educated, circumspect statesmen who would promote the particular interests of their states while honoring and protecting the Constitution and the system it chartered. And again, they were selected by legislatures, meaning that higher quality people were selected and filtered out until the best remained. The entire process created incentives to protect and promote this arrangement, making it self-sustaining and insular in the best ways.

This is a process that brings to mind Washington's anecdote about the purpose of the Senate. The anecdote goes like this: Washington had breakfast with Jefferson one day, and the topic of the upper chamber came up. What was the role of the Senate, exactly, Jefferson wanted to know? In response, George

Washington is said to have told Jefferson the Senate's role is to "cool" House legislation as a saucer was used to cool hot tea.[28]

The result was a chamber filled with people both above and involved in politics; they advocated for their home states and constituents within a larger structure that they also valued and whose rules they were attuned to. And it was the better chamber in Congress: it steered the institution's course and adroitly managed its—and the nation's—affairs via its role as the final check on high-level personnel, both in the president's cabinet and on the federal courts.

To reiterate this essential point, a big reason why the Senate succeeded to such a high degree in remaining focused on what it was chartered to do (protecting the interests of the *states* as political actors and the Constitution) without degrading over time was because it was insulated from politics. Since its members were not concerned with elections and appealing to the media and their narratives, ignorant voters, hardcore partisans, etc., its members could focus on prioritizing good governance over getting reelected.

Some may dismiss this argument on the grounds that it is insufficiently pro-democracy, which I think is a mistake. Consider the following. People forget that, like the rest of us, our elected representatives are only human. There are certain things they can and cannot do, and their time and attention are limited. As such, incentive structures matter because they funnel people towards certain tasks. The genius of the original Constitution was that it ensured that the Senate would be filled with smart, capable people, while nudging them to focus on their constitutionally-ordained responsibilities. The upshot is that this non-democratic arrangement maximized the common good of managing America's internal affairs.

Sadly (and ironically), the passage of the Seventeenth Amendment estranged senators from the local politics and interests of their states by subjecting them to elections and in turn to the whims of the people, whose opinions and interests are formed more by media, groupthink, interest groups, prejudices, and national political figures than any idea of national interest or institutional restraint. Moreover, democratizing the Senate homogenized and weakened it as an institution, which again, empowered other elements in the federal government and necessarily undermined federalism in America. With elections as the new focus, both houses of Congress were happy to defer many of their responsibilities to the Executive Branch. (We discuss this problem in depth in later chapters.)

It is my opinion that the cumulative effects of these amendments set in motion the collapse of the original Constitution and paved the way for its successor in the form of the New Deal legal regime that came to the fore in the following decades. Progressivism did not arrive overnight; the situation its activists capitalized on was the result of years of work. Much of the damage was done through two amendments—the Sixteenth and Seventeenth—that made the government larger, graft a bigger issue, and empowered opinion-forming institutions (e.g., universities and the media) while weakening the federal system that had existed to that point.

In short, Washington, D.C. became *the place* where politics happened in the US. Massive flows of cash flooded the administrative zone situated on the marshy lands beside the Potomac River, making it much swampier and a Mecca of sorts for special interests. This marsh of corruption slowly built up atop the old regime, and it eventually buried the original Constitution.

A New Coat of Paint:
Filling out the Progressive Constitution

By the time the progressives came to power under President Wilson, and again and more dramatically under President Franklin Roosevelt, the structures of American government and law had already been weakened and rearranged, meaning they were ready to be fully torn down and largely rebuilt. Power was concentrated in Washington, D.C., and the impact that the government had on everyday life was large and growing; the original Constitution had been nearly supplanted by counterproductive amendments, and in other cases its text was ignored outright; and the arrival of the modern democratic age suggested more radical changes were incoming.

FDR's infamous (and successful) intimidation of the Supreme Court, the adoption of a more explicitly political, outcome-oriented jurisprudence by the justices, and the birth of the Administrative State[29]—important as these events were, they more marked the finishing touches on a protracted project than a sudden revolution of their own. The progressives built a new political regime in the previous decades; by the 1930s, they were simply applying their preferred final aesthetic touches.

If the original Constitution was a charter for a limited government, then the new Constitution was a permission for expansive state intervention in markets and civil society. Some might think this sounds ridiculous, but when I was in law school, it became clear to me that this is more or less exactly how things work in practice. A straightforward way to think about the contrast between the two constitutional systems is with a hypothetical. Consider the following.

Let us say that you are in court challenging some government action. Under the original Constitution, the government would need to provide reasons for why it was taking some action, and the presumption would be *against* its arguments; it would need to find some textual justification for its actions. In other words, the law would bend towards the individual.

Under the progressive Constitution, however, the text would be far less important. Instead, you—the person opposed to the government's actions—would be required to present some reason as to why it could *not* engage in some regulatory activity. The new Constitution basically puts the old one on its head, and its thumb on the scale to favor the state.

The underlying principle of the progressive Constitution is the idea that the government should have the power to "fix" (or to try to ameliorate) nationwide problems. If the state is oriented towards those goals, then everything nominally provided by the Constitution by way of rights protections is negotiable. Legal decisions have followed from this proposition, with the formation of the Administrative State being the crowning achievement of this development.

A host of different, legally dubious, and functionally unaccountable departments and agencies were established by Executive Order and/or by Congress during the depressions of the 1930s and 1940s (to mitigate economic dislocations), in the 1950s and 1960s (to outlaw disparate treatment under the law), and in the decades since to police civil society and to engage in social engineering (to enforce liberal attitudes and outlaw conservative opinions in business and academia, among other things).[30] Many of these entities enjoy rule-making powers, as well as the ability to reach and enforce their own decisions. The separation of powers—once the centerpiece of the American system—is irrelevant in these administrative courts, which is a microcosm of sorts for the larger decline of the law in American life.

Bureaucrats have never been stronger and federal elections have never mattered less. Though it's sad to admit, even conservative presidents celebrated today, including Reagan, did virtually nothing to slow the growth of the federal behemoth; needless to say, they could not limit its power or influence, let alone push back against the New Deal constitution. There is a direct line from these failures to the abuse of American citizens and America First politicians in the present day. The Deep State has been around for a long time, and it is only now openly throwing its weight around.

As an aside, I must mention that some conservatives look back fondly on the Deep State for its involvement in the Cold War against the Soviets. One can debate the merits of that argument, but it is clear that those methods and attitudes survived the conflict and increasingly operate in a domestic political situation that is unjust and deeply concerning. The FISA Court saga, which was marked by a clandestine paranoia during the Trump years, demonstrates this problem in full.[31] But again, there are myriad instances of this at the DOD, Treasury, and elsewhere.

Let's return to a previously discussed point, that Executive Branch initiatives by the Deep State only go in one direction, i.e., to the Left. As we saw with President Trump, career employees will sabotage presidential initiatives unless they are progressive in their orientation. And in my own tenure at EPA, I saw how Executive Branch employees do what they can to undermine policies and presidents who they dislike. The legality here is irrelevant; they do what they want because they can get away with it. They are aware of this and act accordingly.

Some so-called conservatives deny that there is a Deep State—by which I simply mean the illegal and partisan behavior of the bureaucrats who constitute the Administrative State, which I would hope all conservatives acknowledge is real and a problem—and say that the reason that President Trump was handicapped was due to his character or personnel, or perhaps some other factor or combination of factors. Others say that, because the Deep State isn't arresting people in the middle of the night (though that is starting to happen, albeit in the early morning hours rather than at midnight), then the name doesn't fit.[32]

This may be so, but I think blaming Trump to avoid the discomfort of admitting that we live under a partisan legal regime (i.e., one that is outcome-oriented and unfair) is a pretty lame and unconvincing argument. (And as I will discuss later, there is a reason that the Deep State has become more prominent in recent years.) It also avoids the issue of the bureaucracy reinforcing its ideology and helping its allies to fight reform efforts, e.g., union dues are put towards electing Democrats in Congress who will reflexively support partisans in the Executive Branch.[33]

Whatever one thinks of President Trump, all conservatives and Republicans should be able to look at the problems he identified and agree that they are problems. If you don't share that view, then, you might be a Democrat.

Realism and Reform

There are so many different anecdotes to pick from to show how this asymmetrical legal-illegal problem penetrates all aspects of our new constitutional system, and how it goes back to the bureaucracy. I will limit myself to one example, which happens

to be one of the most compelling. Look at civil rights law. This
category of the legal code is meant to protect individuals from disparate treatment because of their race, gender, age, and a handful
of other criteria. The text of the most authoritative laws explicitly
outlaw discrimination on the basis of race.[34]

And how does it work in practice? The US at the federal level,
via the Executive Branch bureaucracy, promotes and defends a
robust, all-encompassing affirmative action regime that would
make the old USSR's "nationalities policies" look tame.[35] Racial
preferences are everywhere because they must be: the application
of civil rights law by government agencies and administrators
functionally mandates businesses and universities employ HR/DEI
(Diversity, Equity, and Inclusion) officers and adhere to an explicit
racial spoils system. Merit, testing, metrics—all are thrown out in
the name of progressive social-engineering. And there is a lot of
money in this cottage industry.

But it only goes in one direction, which is in favor of the groups
progressives use for political gain, meaning women, homosexuals,
and blacks (occasionally they throw a bone to immigrants, but
increasingly they get tossed into the least-favored nations category along with East Asians, South Asians, and Caucasians). This
means that disparate treatment of those categories of people is
A-okay. But anything in the other direction is actionable.

As a reminder: The 1964 Civil Rights Act—the key law
which was upheld and amplified by the Supreme Court numerous
times—explicitly bans this practice. There is supposed to be one
law for everyone. But it doesn't matter. If progressives want to create and advance an American caste system, commandeer private
industries through the HR office, and remake civil society with the
iron fist of the state, then that is fine. The Administrative State will

allow and encourage it. Indeed, progressives in the bureaucracy have done all of this for decades, and even today, conservatives in Congress seem only mildly concerned.

The results are striking. In only a generation, the firms of private companies have moved decidedly to the Left, and even more concerning, many Americans are organizing themselves by race because they understand that the new constitutional regime we live under allocates benefits and distributes penalties based on racial identity.[36]

All of this emanates from the law and its enforcement by the bureaucracy. To be sure, there are many non-partisan, mission-driven civil servants. But the overall ethos of the permanent bureaucracy is left-wing, which helps to explain this sustained, potent, and partisan problem.

In the 1980s, President Reagan began to move at some of these issues and he was thoroughly rebuked by the powers that be in D.C., and backed off.[37] Since then, only President Trump has expressed any interest in reforming this gargantuan racket. Sadly, he had little success. At the same time, a majority of Americans oppose these practices. But public opinion means little when it comes to the actions of the Executive Branch.

In my view, this gets to the heart of the issue with the Deep State: it simply cannot be tamed because it is outside the control of Congress and voters (though the former is a choice). The bureaucracy as an institution is chiefly a creation of the New Deal constitution, making it an extension of and a connection to the larger swamp; it is the estuary, and the Deep State is immediately downstream. But what really matters is acknowledging that the entire river system is polluted.

The Administrative State is omnipresent and reactive to conservative reformers—something we saw during the farcical first impeachment of President Trump, and which progressives openly admit to.[38] So far, all attempts to tame it get the attention of the Deep State bureaucrats who go into overdrive. The entire institution is progressive and it cannot be checked by a Congress that is pusillanimous at best. When one realizes that the lobbying-contracting complex is a further buffer against the election of representatives who might take the problem seriously, the entire situation becomes darker.

The key takeaway is this: Progressives are very good at capturing institutions and insulating them from reforms. Just think about the Supreme Court. This was the first institution progressives captured, and it took more than sixty years to begin to take it back.[39] Winning back lost territory is *very* difficult to do in politics because of the institutional advantages progressives possess (money, media, etc.). Amending broken institutions is *very* difficult to do. The path of least resistance is best, and that translates to minimizing the Administrative State through the removal of its employees and the narrowing of its mission, a plan that I expand on in later chapters.

The Deep State Drones

To this point, we have discussed the rise of the Administrative/Deep State, the ways in and the degree to which it conquered the Constitution, and its malicious role in everyday life, and especially in politics and markets. While we have talked about the politics of these people (they are doctrinaire progressives), we have said very little to this point about the particular people and the specific views they hold on policy.

In the coming section, I talk a bit about the enduring nature of this competition between conservatives, moderates, constitutionalists, what have you, and their progressive opponents. As we will see, the rivalry has developed, but over time, we have struggled to counter the ascent of the progressives and their capture of institutions. A big reason for this insurmountable challenge is due to the common ideology of bureaucrats, which in turn has helped to expand the reach of the Deep State.

Afterwards, I will discuss the use of NGOs and legally questionable international agreements by progressives to secure policy outcomes that they cannot obtain even within a system oriented towards furthering their goals. The swamp is deep and the Administrative State is a tricky beast. Studying all of its aspects is essential if we are to take it apart. The next chapter begins with an assessment of the bureaucrats who run the machine before looking at what they have achieved, and what they hope to achieve in the future. In this chapter, we saw how the structure of the Deep State took form. Next, we will look at its agents, their missions, where their power comes from, and how it is used against reform efforts.

CHAPTER 3

EXECUTIVE BRANCH ANARCHY

The Sources of Progressive Power

In the last chapter, we examined the history of the swamp and gave an account of how certain well-intentioned but harmful amendments to the Constitution produced unforeseen developments that led to a constitutional revolution. This was a radical transformation in government, and the culmination of this process—the arrival of the New Deal constitution—necessitated, and indeed demanded, the establishment of a permanent bureaucratic class.[40] Without that class, there are reasons to believe that the larger progressive project would collapse.

This was a massive change, though it isn't widely studied in schools. Unsurprisingly, many informed conservatives may not appreciate its significance. Something I often point out to conservatives who are frustrated with the one-sidedness of politics in D.C. is this: we don't live under the original Constitution anymore.

The next step is seeing that the usurper progressive constitution is not neutral. Realizing that it is partisan and unsurprisingly moves in a particular ideological direction helps to explain the feeling that the process is rigged, because in an important sense, it is. Where the original Constitution was a neutral document, its successor is outcome-oriented.[41] At the same time, this fact also clarifies why it is that the government in Washington attracts and produces career workers who are decidedly on the Left: the Executive Branch of today is a product of that progressive constitution.[42]

The last point I want to make before jumping into the discussion at a higher level is that the final outcome of this decades-long constitutional revolution was the formation of the Administrative State. The Administrative State is the living and reactive soul of the New Deal Constitution, and its Deep State drones—the partisans who flagrantly transcend the law to retain and expand its power—are the last line of defense against reform. Unfortunately, so far, they've done a great job on that end.

In this chapter, we will talk in detail about the people who constitute the partisan resistance to reform within the Executive Branch, as well as examine their relationship to the many institutional barriers to reform. Much of this section will look specifically at the ways in which career employees can and do undermine conservative goals and sow chaos in our politics when the *status quo* is threatened. But any serious investigation must acknowledge a few basic but salient truths about progressive power within the Administrative State.

How the Cycle Repeats

A lot has been written about the different psychological traits of conservatives and liberals, and how those inclinations often influence worldviews and life decisions, including where one works and what one does.[43] A joke with a great deal of truth to it, and which I assume many are somewhat familiar with, is that conservatives like to make money while liberals like to make rules. I think that axiom is largely true and would add that the other important fact is that liberals are far more united *internally* than conservatives are.

It used to be that conservatism in America was a stool with three legs (social conservatives, economic libertarians, and defense hawks); in contrast, liberals have a single united chair. Distinct views on interests and unique groupings have serious implications for how these two political groups operate when it comes to making decisions in and around government. While there have always been divisions within the conservative tent, those differences are becoming more prominent—a point I will return to in later chapters. But their existence at all has created some friction and made governing less fluid, particularly at the federal level.

Liberals, and especially progressives, are willing to accept broad proclamations regarding causes of certain problems (e.g., racism or the current phobia their friends in the media and the academy are railing about) whereas conservatives are more internally disagreeable and disunited on a host of questions, from immigration to foreign policy.

The reason that this matters is because liberal unity helps to solidify interests around certain issues; it also allows liberals to accumulate power and to establish lasting influence within institutions, including the Executive Branch. Conservatives, in contrast, face an uphill battle with the bureaucracy—and that is to say nothing of the internal challenges. And in my own experience I have seen why, and much of it comes from the fact that conservatives do not share a general outlook on political problems and solutions, which hurts our ability to unite to impact lasting change.

I say all of this not to critique conservatives or to praise liberals. On the contrary, I bring this up to help explain the longevity of the Administrative State, as well as the unique threat it presents:

It is an ideologically-grounded entity, and one consequently with staying power as well as the capacity to protect itself and to grow. While conservatives argue and deliberate among themselves, the Administrative State works to further entrench itself and its interests.

This should not be new information. Conservatives have long understood this reality. To see the proof of this, just look back on one of the most important speeches delivered by an American conservative since 1950.

In 1980, Ronald Reagan, who was then running for office, told a crowd at the Neshoba County Fair that "a government bureaucracy, no matter how well-intentioned, [has as] its top priority . . . preservation of the bureaucracy."[44] Bureaucracies, like all organisms, are self-interested, meaning they want to grow and survive, and they are good at that (just think about what Reagan is saying—his problems then remain our problems today, only they're worse with the passage of time).

Furthermore, what is true of the whole is true of the parts. Bureaucrats have their own individual goals, as well as larger group tasks. They want to see their efforts rewarded, and they do not want their pet projects to disappear when they leave. They are focused on building legacies, and the smarter ones are very good at this by creating incentives and rules to sustain projects into the future.

Bureaucratic self-interest is one important reason why it is so difficult to shut down outdated offices, to rewrite pointless rules, and to engage in even the most modest of reforms within the Executive Branch. The most informed people are also the most ingrained, so they can do all manner of things to preserve their programs, goals, etc. I know that this issue exists throughout the

Executive Branch, which should give an idea of the enormity of the problem.

For progressive ideologues whose policies can be pushed onto everyday Americans, this is especially true. And in practice, this means that they have powerful reasons to mold and perfect their offices, projects, teams, organizations, and rules to guarantee longevity, especially when faced with attempts at reform.

Crucially, they also have the capacity to do so. The law awards contracts to the allies of progressives;[45] they can also hire ideologically aligned employees[46] and settle lawsuits with like-minded advocacy groups to pay allies and to implement certain rules.[47] They can also leak information[48] to facilitate investigations, bring enforcement actions,[49] and direct federal money to the campaigns of progressives via union dues.

Put bluntly, Conservatives are in an asymmetrical fight within the Executive Branch, as we don't have the ability to do most of these things, let alone the knowhow. In a very real sense, we reformers are fighting a political battle with an arm tied behind our back—though this doesn't begin to capture the scale of our disadvantage.

Furthermore, these are but a few techniques among a much larger arsenal of options available to partisans in the Executive Branch, most of which derive from the fact that progressives have deep wells of institutional knowledge to draw from, as well as infrastructure of their own design to hide behind when dealing with reformers.

All of this is possible primarily because of the continuity of progressive thought on various issues that make governing at the federal level far easier. Again, this cooperation means that they are well-suited to do this and to continue doing this over time because they don't need to explain their mission to their replacement(s)—they already know what's going on.

The few conservative civil servants in the Executive Branch, however, are not nearly as synchronized or forward-looking, which helps to explain why they have failed to both establish a political foothold and to exert ideological pressure. They also play by the rules, which cannot always be said for their rivals.

To return to the Reagan anecdote, I would be remiss not to comment on the point I alluded to in Chapter 2, namely that American conservatives have been locked in a long, slowly failing war against the bureaucracy—even if they didn't know it at the time. As mentioned in the previous chapter, conservatives were able to ignore some of the troubling aspects of the Administrative State and its Deep State goons because of the efforts against foreign communists during the Cold War, i.e., they turned their focus abroad at foreign enemies with whom they disagreed.[50]

But today, they can no longer afford to turn their eyes away from that fact because the Deep State is no longer working against the enemies of America. Rather, it is fighting the domestic opponents of the progressive project that gave it life last century.[51] Conservatives must wake up to this reality and confront these abuses in a forceful, meaningful way.

This is especially true and timely because, as I stated above, progressivism is a coherent ideology with minimal internal dissent, meaning that, like a boulder rolling down a hill, once it gets going, it is hard to stop. Given how long it's been going, there should be heightened concern to retard its movement further lest we lose all capacity to institute the reforms needed to defeat the usurper constitution of the 1930s.

All of this brings me to the conclusion of this subsection, namely that, just as there is a Deep State, there is also a larger progressive program. Guided by ideology, this list of goals exists, is lofty, and can be implemented (with disastrous consequences). It must be stopped.

Conservatives must be cognizant of the fact that, whatever polling might suggest, the progressive movement has growing influence, in no small part because they dominate the Democratic Party and set the agenda. Put differently, while low-income voters in South Carolina may determine who wins the Democratic nomination, it's the professional governing class that decides on policy questions. The upshot is that nothing will change radically either way; progressives always rule.

And who are these people? Broadly speaking, they are the MAs, JDs, and others with specified knowledge that they can draw on in their day-to-day work within the Executive Branch. Many have obvious ties to Democratic politics while others worked in media or higher education. The revolving door between Democratic administrations, the academy, and career roles in the Executive Branch gives this cohort the power to influence and impact policy at a geometric rate over time.

During Republican Administrations, they stall; when Democrats have the White House, they put their feet on the gas. The result is that they are able to successfully push left-wing politics on everyday Americans via the various departments in the federal government and to stifle reform.

All of this partisanship, ideology, money, and knowledge positions progressives well to network and assemble capable teams for the various political roles that open up to a new administration; it also guarantees that they'll remain in power even when a Republican occupies the Executive Branch. As it stands, progressives own the federal government. Unless things change, they always will—which will mean that federal elections will continue to mean little for Republicans.

At the Pleasure of the President

Make no mistake about it, professional progressives run the show in the Executive Branch. I personally saw a lot of this up close at the EPA. GS-14s and GS-15s would utilize their institutional knowledge and capacity to frustrate the rule-making process, to mislead us, and to guarantee that whatever the previous administration had done, it would not be easily undone. Without equal knowledge, we were often led around in circles. Given the time constraints a president faces, this stalling tactic can be extremely destructive.

This is a crucially important point, because it shows that the "Administrative Threat"[52] as the esteemed legal scholar Philip Hamburger called it, goes well beyond what happened in Bonn and even the issues President Trump faced over four years in office, e.g., the revolt at the National Security Council,[53] disloyalty at the Department of Justice, etc.[54] (None of the individuals who broke the law were ever punished, which is a problem in its own right that gets further coverage later in the book.) It is a comprehensive and systemic problem that threatens the law-making process and the rights of all citizens.

Put bluntly, this conflict has its origins *within* the Executive Branch, and is an all-encompassing problem that is inextricably at odds with the Constitution and the rule of law. The reason is simple: Those in the Executive Branch do not work for popularly elected presidents—that is, unless you're a liberal Democrat. This is unacceptable for the simple reason that it negates the effects and processes of American democracy.

The fundamental starting point for all things Executive Branch is the truth that those in this segment of the federal government work for the president. They do not work for themselves, their pet projects, or even the people (at least not directly). Rather, that is the role of the president, who is elected by voters; it is these people who shape the president's agenda. It is up to him and all those under him to carry out that mandate *as the president sees fit*.

This arrangement is the whole reason elections matter: the president works for the people, yes, *but he especially works for the people who elected him.* Their interests matter most in a sense because they determine who will occupy the Executive Branch for the next four years. Progressives dispute this, and given their influence in the Executive Branch, there is little that changes with federal elections.

The only way this situation works is if the president is the head honcho, the boss, and the ultimate decider of how the Executive Branch functions, lest the permanent state implement its will without recourse. In fact, the president *is* the Executive Branch in the sense that he must oversee and sign off on its actions. This is an indivisible office; all that is there is the president in the decision-making process. Progressives unsurprisingly reject this truth.

For example, during President Trump's term in office, his Attorney General, Bill Barr, noted that the president is a "unitary executive"[55]—a fancy legal way of saying that the president controls the Executive Branch. To be sure, the branch gets its funding from Congress in many cases, and is bound by the decisions of the Supreme Court, but the office itself *is* the president.

What is notable about the progressive argument against the unity of the Executive Branch is that it is one of the few times that they will contend that there are limits on the power of the president. The reason for this is stated above: they take this view because, when they're out of office, they want a weaker Executive Branch, or at least one in which the component parts can be autonomous and frustrate the Republican president. Of course, they never argue this when a Democrat is in the White House.

The discussion to this point is a roundabout path to one of the most important contentions in the book, namely that those within the Executive Branch *must* serve at the pleasure of the president if they are to truly serve the president. To reiterate: this is because action by the Executive Branch is and must be an expression of the president's will. This goes for everyone, and it is particularly true for those who have policy-related roles (think about the GS-14s and GS-15s I discussed above) in which their jobs can and do impact the implementation of specific policies.

There is a direct democratic chain from the decisions that voters make to the rules that are implemented by presidents. Executive Branch employees are a part of that chain, but they are passive actors, responding to and acting in accordance with the decisions of voters and their selected representative in the White House.

This all-important arrangement is a core aspect of our democratic system. Sadly, as those who paid attention from 2016 to 2021 already know, this chain visibly broke down in the worst ways during President Trump's tenure. Bureaucrats across the government decided that they could not allow the duly elected president to execute the duties to which voters entrusted him.

The "silent majority" as Trump called it—or "flyover country" as liberals derided it—could not have a say in the direction of the country, progressives determined, so they took extralegal steps to undermine the new government. Many of those actions have been referenced above, but if I wanted to document all of those wrongs, I would be writing an encyclopedia, not this book. Indeed, "the resistance" began *before* President Trump was even elected via the Russia Hoax, or IntelGate as it should be known, given the involvement of America's "national security" agencies in initiating and spreading the conspiracy.[56]

This entire saga was an outrageous *coup* orchestrated by the Clinton Campaign and holdover officials from the Obama Administration. For our discussion, the key point is that this unlawful resistance had its genesis in the Executive Branch. To prevent crises like this in the future, we must assert the primacy of the president in the Executive Branch by stating loudly and reaffirming that those in his employment serve him, not their own interests.

This is only possible if these employees can be accountable to the president, which in turn means that he must be able to terminate their employment if and when they disobey him. (There should also be a means of holding lawbreakers accountable, but that is a problem for a later chapter.) The corollary is that he must be able to hire his own people in any and all policy-influencing roles should he need to.

But as it stands, there is no such mechanism for gaining control over the Administrative State, and thus no way to limit the Deep State's dirty tricks. This is not to say that there are no means of asserting control, however. In the next section, I discuss a few of the impediments that have given Republicans fits before turning to some of the solutions available to serious reformers.

Why Haven't Things Changed?

All things considered, the Republicans have done a great job electorally at the federal level since Harry Truman left office. Notwithstanding the poor electoral showing the last two decades, Republicans have consistently been in close competition for the White House most of the last seventy years;[57] and since dissolving the Democrats' once-unbreakable hold on the House of Representatives,[58] they've done quite well in Washington, D.C., at least in terms of wins and losses.

Where they have not done well, however, is in implementing institutional reforms. As noted above, Republicans are at a serious disadvantage when it comes to navigating the Executive Branch, and thus cannot control it in any meaningful way. Unsurprisingly, they haven't been particularly effective at changing it, either. The result is a sad one: many Republican voters feel that their votes have been worthless, that their representatives have failed to impact change.[59]

There is some truth to that, even when looking at the two most celebrated Republican presidents, Reagan and Trump respectively. Reagan failed to curtail the growth of government;[60] he also failed to eliminate the Department of Education—his archnemesis on the campaign trail.[61]

President Trump was similarly vexed when it came to draining the swamp, though he encountered a handful of novel problems, chief among them the COVID-19 pandemic.[62] Both men were enacted to reform D.C., and neither succeeded. Sadly, many more Republican presidents have made almost no attempt at all.

Based on my experiences and my research, there are several challenges Republicans face in overcoming the Administrative State and implementing the reforms necessary to transform Washington.

We already discussed one of them, namely the permanent bureaucracy and the knowledge and institutions it uses to blunt reforms and to assist progressive causes. Being led in circles is a real problem, and so is running into weaponized rules and administrators. Overcoming subsidized advocacy groups and a biased New Deal Constitution are two more hurdles.

The second problem is ignorance. Many Republicans don't have a vision for what is possible and remain politically ignorant (this is sometimes a choice). They opt for the superficial and fleeting rather than engaging in the arduous task of planning and executing substantive reforms.

In this case, they are no better than the Congressional Republicans who engage in moral grandstanding and theatre (or play along with Democrats who engage in it) by voting to condemn ancient wrongs, universally recognized villains, etc.[63] rather than doing their constitutionally-designated jobs. Too many Republican appointees in the Executive Branch are content to go through the motions of actually governing, and that is unacceptable.

The third issue is one that Republicans everywhere struggle with: standing up to the media and ignoring their pressure campaigns. Some Republicans who serve in the Executive Branch are great; they have big ideas, want to make a difference, and even know how to bring about change. Many of these people run on being fighters to get elected, and some genuinely are.

But at the last second, they back off. Typically, this is because of a critical hit piece or an attack on their character by the *Washington Post* or *New York Times*, or perhaps a rant on MSNBC. I feel for people in this category because I know that bad press can hurt, but serving your country is a bigger calling, and those under attack must push through to achieve greatness.

The fourth barrier is yet another doozy: a lack of assistance by other conservative entities. It's well-known that Congress cannot be counted on to do its job,[64] so it's no surprise that it hasn't helped out in efforts to reform the Executive Branch. What is less known is that the courts have been counterproductive in this space as well. The bending of the law to weaken Republican presidents goes back decades. Still, it was on display in the Trump years,[65] and it underscores an unfortunate reality: reformers in the Executive Branch must plan to lead the way internally, as there is unlikely to be any external assistance by way of draining the swamp.

In sum, there are a host of impediments to conservatives who want to reform Washington, D.C. To this point, the situation may look grim. But it shouldn't. To paraphrase Richard Hanania, a libertarian social scientist with a conservative bent, Republicans have not yet begun to fight for control of government. There are so many things that we can do to take on the swamp. And all of those efforts begin with the will to try.

Blueprints and Backbones

So, what can be done to assert control over the Executive Branch, and in turn the government in America? The answer is, quite a lot, even if Congressional Republicans are disinterested in governing and reform.

Throughout the remainder of the book, I will discuss the low-hanging fruit, the most realistic and indeed most impactful options available to us when it comes to impacting substantive reforms at the federal level. In the broadest sense, those options boil down to the below topics:

- Reforming the civil service classification process
- Hiring brave, capable leaders on the appointee side
- Revisiting and reversing the rules that give progressives institutional advantages in governing and elections

These are admittedly somewhat nebulous topics, but in the coming chapters I will expound on what each of these categories means. As will become clear, they are all intimately related and equally important. I firmly believe that if we can make reforms in these three areas, then we will go a long way in fixing the Executive Branch.

At the same time, we cannot pick and choose; we need to reform all three areas if we are to do what Presidents Reagan and Trump attempted to do, namely to make fundamental changes to the rotten institutions in D.C. and to the culture that sustains that rot.

Optimism and resolve are essential to our goal as conservative reformers. Cliche as it has become, being a happy warrior is a must if we are to make the changes that the conservative movement has promised for decades. We must also be sure of ourselves and loyal to our plans. Governing requires meticulous planning, intense determination, and a unity of message and purpose. These elements have been missing in too many Republican governments, which has contributed to the common outcome.

Now, let's turn to the actual template to drain the swamp. These plans begin with a discussion about a little-known but potent idea that nearly took effect during President Trump's term.

CHAPTER 4

YOU'RE FIRED

A World Without Consequences

With the 2024 Republican primaries underway, some in the press have begun to ask who the Donald Trump of this cycle might be, i.e., the outsider to catch fire. In my view, the 2016 Trump phenomenon is unlikely to be replicated for the simple reason that Donald Trump was a singular candidate because he was a national figure well before he ever ran for office.

Sure, he was ubiquitous in the tabloids and on talk radio; he appeared in a few movies, too. But the real reason that everyone knew Trump was because of his hilarious, multi-season television series, *The Apprentice*. The premise is straightforward: people compete in teams for Trump's affections and support by participating in zany challenges; at the end of each episode, someone gets eliminated.

In typical Trump fashion, the show was known for the future president's showmanship. And that was captured in his now-famous catchphrase, "You're fired!" *The Apprentice* is must-see reality TV, and it holds up.

I'm a big fan of *The Apprentice*, and I think that the basic premise of rewarding good behavior and punishing bad behavior is a great lesson, and one with applicability beyond the realm of entertainment and business. And I'm not alone in thinking that there is a virtue in firing people for messing up.

Towards the end of the Trump Administration, there were conversations in the White House and with the various agencies about bringing the "You're Fired" ethos to the federal government. At the most basic level, President Trump wanted to bring accountability to the federal government because he understood that, without it, there would be no hope for draining the swamp. As such, he and his team sought to introduce a mechanism for better political control of the Executive Branch—something that is essential if federal elections are to mean anything.

As discussed in the last chapter, it is no easy feat to remove career employees. In another callback, David Bernhardt's *You Report to Me: Accountability for the Failing Administrative State (2023)* provides a comprehensive account of how frustrating and convoluted the firing process is; he details the many tedious hurdles one must clear to remove even the worst employees.[66] Stated bluntly, it is unimaginably difficult to fire someone in the federal government; for political appointees, it *is* impossible to remove subversive and/or badly performing careers. This is completely untenable.

Consequently, federal employees become like so many others in and around government in D.C.: insulated from their failures and free to transgress rules and norms as they like. The trouble is that being able to remove career employees is sometimes essential for political appointees, particularly when they are being insubordinate or useless. But there are a host of other instances in which termination is equally valid, e.g., when they do things that would result in being fired in any other enterprise, such as engaging in sexual harassment, failing to assist on projects, or simply refusing to do their work altogether.

But regrettably, firing bad employees and poor performers is not that simple in the federal government. A labyrinthian assortment of rules and procedures, as well as powerful unions, make the removal of even the most poorly behaved federal employee a challenge. To make matters worse, the "solution" is often simply to move these people, meaning that they incur no real economic cost for their bad behavior; they continue to get paid well and typically hold onto their pensions. The upshot is that there are no real negative consequences for screwing up. Others see this and act accordingly, e.g., at the FBI. This is a flatly unjust situation.

The manifest issues with the current situation—the most obvious and pernicious of them being that Executive Branch employees get the unwarranted privilege of living in a world without consequences, which no doubt incentivizes and reinforces partisan behavior and sloth—became clear to me after the Bonn fiasco. From that point forward, I was committed to reforming this broken system.

Fixing this dysfunctional process was the crux of the plan to bring "you're fired" to the Executive Branch. James Sherk, an economist with a focus on labor and employment law, offered a great starting point to reforming the federal government's backwards termination regime (or lack thereof).

Sherk's solution was the Schedule F designation. This rule would give the president the ability to alter the designations of certain career employees—those with a substantive impact on policy—to Schedule F, which in turn would give the head of the Executive Branch the ability to reassign and remove these subordinates, including and especially those who would not work for him.[67]

In short, this new categorization would provide the president with the basic ability to inform badly behaved careers that they would be fired rather than shuffled around to another agency or department, or even tolerated in their existing role. This plan, if implemented, would revolutionize the civilian workforce while also solidifying the president's constitutionally ordained power to lead the Executive Branch. All the plan required was an Executive Order by President Trump, which he signed late in his tenure.[68]

Unsurprisingly, once the plan began to circulate, the media and other Democrats went insane.[69] The idea that a Republican president could force the bureaucracy to do its job by executing his or her will was too much for progressives in D.C. to fathom. Many lied and said that the Executive Branch cannot be politicized by Republicans by creating the power to remove career employees—which is a funny argument because the Executive Branch is meant to execute the political goals of whoever wins the White House. It's only politicized in the negative sense when it refuses to serve the elected president.

These progressive partisans also frequently asserted that the Schedule F designation was unnecessary. Badly behaved employees are already subject to penalties and discipline, they claimed. Setting aside the fallout from the Bonn nightmare, I am confident that a brief review of the record shows that assertion to be false. All too often, the badly behaved get off; and when they are held accountable, it is usually only out of sheer luck. Simply consider the infamous case of John Beale.

EPA's Agent 007

The Coen Brothers are two of the greatest filmmakers in history. While they are best known for films like *Fargo* (1996) and *The Big Lebowski* (1998), *Burn After Reading* (2008) is another excellent movie by the duo. The premise of the comedy-*cum-faux*-thriller is that people in D.C. are self-absorbed and obsessed with the mystique of government service; it also hilariously points out that their behavior is absurdly affected, typically to give the impression of importance.

The story isn't based on true events, but one of its subplots does have parallels to the real-world case of John Beale. Beale was a military veteran with numerous degrees who was hired as a Senior Policy Advisor to the EPA at the GS-15 level; he was a highly paid and well-regarded expert with impeccable credentials.[70] In short, he was the perfect candidate for the federal government. Once hired, Beale was viewed as effective by his colleagues, and he worked on important national projects.

Though Beale was well-compensated for his work, it evidently wasn't enough for him. At the same time Beale was at the EPA, he began to take time off during the workday to do classified work for the CIA. He informed his superiors of this, but due to the nature of his work, he couldn't say much more. The only problem is that none of this was true.

Growing more brazen with the passage of time, Beale would go on to lie about his medical history to get subsidized benefits; he demanded reimbursement for personal trips that he presented as work-related; and would eventually altogether stop showing up for work for months at a time while he was "working" for the CIA.

Despite the absurdity and shamelessness of his antics, Beale might have gotten away with it. Indeed, the only reason he was ultimately caught was because he *was still getting paid* for active work well into his retirement. Even a nice retirement plan wasn't enough. At long last, the entire charade was uncovered.

This 007 was finally caught and the justice system ultimately prevailed: Beale was convicted, sentenced, and jailed for his lies and for his fraud against the American people. The scope of his misdeeds is hard to appreciate, but it becomes clear when one learns that he was forced to write a check for almost $1m that he stole from taxpayers.[71]

I thought a lot about Beale when I was at EPA—in no small part because I sat in the office that was once his. Ultimately, he was only brought to justice out of luck, and that is unacceptable. One reason that his fraud went on for as long as it did is because the EPA, like so many departments, is immense and necessarily hard to oversee. The lack of internal political control, the disinterest of Congress, and the absence of a culture of ownership and responsibility make bad actors hard to trace and wrongdoing difficult to uncover.

What makes this all more worrisome is that Beale was an extremely prominent and powerful figure at EPA. Case in point: when he retired, he was making more money than even the administrator—all while pretending to be James Bond to avoid work and responsibility.[72] The salary alone should have raised the antennas of other employees, careers, and political appointees. Someone with that title and responsibilities who was making that kind of money ought to be well-known and involved in the day-to-day work. Instead, Beale was a shadowy figure; he was able to literally disappear—sometimes for months at a time.

I suspect there are many, many cases like Beale's that are never discovered or rectified. I am confident that many lower-level employees get away with similar conduct. What is worse, since COVID-19 hit, many employees throughout the government, including at EPA, have simply stopped showing up for work in person. It's taken years for the federal government to even signal that it might be a good idea to come back to the office.[73]

But rest assured, government workers continue to draw a salary, whether or not they're showing up for work.[74] Just something to think about next time someone in D.C. says that our government employees are underfunded or undermanned.

But the larger point of the Beale episode is that his story speaks to the broad culture of unaccountability that permeates in D.C. generally, and within the Executive Branch in particular. Many employees are self-interested, unhelpful, and liable to cut corners. And given the scope of these agencies and the laxity of the rules for disciplining bad behavior (to the extent that any rules exist at all), the culture that prevails in these institutions is one of smug defiance.

I can attest to this in my interactions with some insubordinate careers. They drag their feet, mislead, and deflect when asked direct, yes-no questions. In short, they behave as if they are above us, and that's because, for all intents and purposes, they are. But that changes with Schedule F, hence the consternation over its implementation.

Another benefit of Schedule F is that it will give political appointees the power to remove BS-ers like Beale. This is not to say it is guaranteed to do so, only that it has the potential to act as a punishment mechanism for the useless as well as the corrupt.

And these are far from the only documented instances of bad behavior at EPA. Infamously, back in 2014, a career employee spent most of his days watching pornography *from his work office on his work computer.*[75] He did this for months on end. In fact, the Inspector General found that he had downloaded over seven thousand files of pornography on his work computer.

For this disgusting misuse of taxpayer money (not to mention his disregard for public decency and a healthy work culture), the culprit was put on leave.[76] In almost any situation in the private sector, the employee would rightly be terminated with few opportunities to appeal the decision. But nope, not in the Executive Branch. Something is deeply wrong in D.C., and while we cannot do much about the general culture of failing upwards, we can and must reform the Executive Branch when and where we can. And the good news is, there is a lot we can do within the Executive Branch to get things on track.

Executive Action in Hiring: The Power to Rescind

Since the New Deal revolution of FDR, government action in D.C. has increasingly come from the president's pen in the form of Executive Orders (EOs).[77] To define them in the most simplistic terms, EOs are powerful documents issued by the president that tell the wider Executive Branch to take a certain action, to hold off from taking action, or to stop doing a specific action altogether. They can be thought of as specific directions intended to get everyone aligned on specific issues.

In my view, EOs have been integral to the transformation of our government, from one of coequal branches to a system in which the Executive Branch dwarfs an impotent Legislative Branch, and which is only sometimes checked by a Judicial Branch that is at least partially handicapped by adhering to the rules of the New Deal constitution. Though this sounds bleak, we should be optimistic: what has been transformed via EO can be changed again by EO.

The Schedule F classification is one type of EO whereby the president can act unilaterally and constitutionally to institute reforms across the federal government when it comes to classification and firing. (To be sure, when instituted—and it must be implemented—Schedule F is certain to trigger massive political and legal battles.) Crucially, the Schedule F EO is not the only substantive presidentially directed reform available when it comes to dealing with personnel. Indeed, there are a host of actions available to the next Republican president via EO that could shift the political playing field in Washington, D.C. by reversing the many actions progressives have taken in the realm of federal hiring.

There is a lot of proverbial low-hanging fruit available to the next Republican president that will go a long way in addressing some of the cultural and institutional problems that have plagued the Executive Branch since they took hold in the 1930s. The reason for this is that a lot of these problems stem from rules on hiring promulgated by EO and left in place by disinterested Republican presidents. The great news is that there is a lot that an interested president can do by EO to change the culture in the federal government if he or she and their team have the resolve.

For instance, the next president could simply rescind bad EOs on hiring that were issued by former presidents. The president can do this for any preexisting EO since they don't have the enduring quality that acts of Congress do. So, what are some EOs to look at?

A good starting point would be to withdraw the many EOs that empower the Equal Employment Opportunity Commission (EEOC) to effectively set the hiring terms of the various departments and federal agencies.[78]

Like so many Civil Rights Era edicts, these EOs—President Nixon's EO 11478 most prominent among them—nominally prevent discrimination in hiring, but in effect demand racial outcomes when it comes to federal personnel. In the time since, the EO has expanded and been amended to require all manner of discrimination in hiring. Curiously, all of these so-called anti-discrimination requirements seem to result in more progressives working in the federal government, many of them with dubious job qualifications. This can and should be easily withdrawn, and it is likely to have a significant effect on the quality and character of the civilian workforce in the Executive Branch.

Another related option would be to rescind Executive Order 11246, which inserts the federal government into the contracts and hiring processes of government contractors, and in doing so demands insanely targeted outcomes that are *de facto* race quotas.[79] This practice was effectively outlawed decades ago in admissions.[80] The Executive Branch needs to catch up.

By a wide margin, Americans reject affirmative action programs and other race-based policies that reward and punish on account of one's ethnic or racial background.[81] Given the Supreme Courts' recent decision on affirmative action, the next Republican president should keep up the momentum and remove race from the world of government contracting.[82]

Affirmative action has a decidedly left-wing orientation—a point that is underscored by the results of polling on the subject.[83] When affirmative action programs are allowed to take effect, they have the power to transform institutions for the worse, which is exactly what happened to academia.[84] Thus, removing racial outcomes-oriented programs from government contracting will have the excellent secondary effect of depoliticizing the enormous and influential cottage industry that has built up around D.C.

Specifically, without rules mandating contractors to be progressive, they will, over time, depoliticize as racial and political considerations move out of the fore. And in turn, these contractors will give less money to progressive ideologues running for Congress, etc. because they won't be in fear of lawsuits and investigations for failing to be in compliance with the D.C. race regime. Obviously, then, this is also a reform that will help to break the cycle of progressives using the government to subsidize their politicians and campaigns.

And these are just the easy options on the issue of hiring in the federal government. So far, we have not said anything about *new* EOs, only reviewed two impactful and bad directives to withdraw. Those topics will be taken up in later chapters.

More Than Just Executive Orders

An Executive Order can go a long way, but we should not have any illusions about its staying power: most of the time, they can and are promptly rescinded by the next president of the opposition party to win the presidency. Consequently, they should be seen as stopgaps or small steps towards more enduring reforms.

At the same time, an EO only works if the president's team is onboard with it and vigorous in its implementation of the directive. This is no problem for Democrats who, as mentioned earlier, are all on the same team when it comes to executing a mission; they are also eager to withdraw EOs from Republican presidents. Republicans are not nearly as synchronized, or as combative; they are happy to go along to get along, which includes leaving in place terrible EOs from their liberal precursors. Even a fighter like President Trump found this out the hard way.

Still, one should not write this off as a problem limited to Trump. On the contrary, one should expect the issue of impotence and disloyalty to be equally frustrating for all Republicans who, like Trump, run on draining the swamp and rooting out corruption in D.C. In fact, I fully anticipate this issue to swell in importance as Republicans become more vocal about reforming the Executive Branch.

Some of President Trump's most prominent and popular EOs were, believe it or not, vigorously opposed by Republicans in his administration. A few that come to mind include his goal of leaving Afghanistan, the effort to remove Diversity, Equity, and Inclusion (DEI) trainings from the federal government, as well as his objective of withdrawing a controversial and crazy Obama Era housing rule that decimated choice and local decision-making about communities and housing.

These were signature Trump issues. Many of these sensible reforms were also bipartisan issues. And yet these efforts were actively thwarted by supposed conservatives in the Trump Administration, some of them at the cabinet-level. These were not career employees; these were political appointees.

This problem is twofold: first, it is a personnel issue—a problem that gets its own discussion in the following chapter; and second, it is one of character. We will save the first half of the issue and address the second aspect here. If you don't have what it takes to serve, then you should not seek out employment in the first place; and if you do make it in, the right thing to do is to resign, not resist. Anything less than that is no different than working as a career and "resisting" Trump, i.e., the constitutional system you swear to uphold when you begin your job.

Serving the president is a privilege, and regrettably, many D.C. Republicans forget that. You are not there to collect a paycheck, to build out your resume, or to attend social events; and you are *definitely* not there to be a speed bump for the president to deal with. We all know the story of the much celebrated "Anonymous"—a low-level staffer at the Department of Homeland Security (DHS) who tried to undercut President Trump; and the stories of DOD and generals lying to Trump to keep the US in Afghanistan are equally well-known.

In all these cases, Republicans were faced with internal disunity and division, problems with their genesis in the sad fact that those they hired to do a job were incapable of doing so. This is a character flaw of the insubordinate first and foremost. Some might reduce this all to issues of talent and ideology on the personnel side of things. But in some cases, those refusing to do their job come from the most respected Republican families.

In my assessment, this gets back to a big problem with Republicans in D.C.: they get absorbed by the progressive culture. This certainly applied to judges like Kennedy and O'Connor on the Supreme Court, or weirdos like Jim Comey at the FBI. But it's much broader than that. It has impacted institutions like the American Enterprise Institute (AEI) and even the more traditionally conservative Heritage Foundation at times.

Believe me, I know it's hard. Staying true to the Constitution in D.C. is a lot like holding onto the Mississippi values I was raised by in a progressive city: it is extremely challenging. I don't deny that. But we must be true to ourselves and relentless in our commitment to those values, and to our obligations.

The upshot is that, when we talk about the power to fire, we need to understand that it should be used judiciously—on career employees and sometimes on badly behaved Republicans, too. A term in office is a short period of time, and given how quickly election cycles arrive, there really isn't time to waste. Hitting the ground running is one thing, but guaranteeing that the machine that is the Executive Branch is still functioning and closing in on goals is equally important.

This is where values and character come in. Beyond having integrity and honesty in working for the president, everyone in the agencies—from principals to careers all the way down through lower-level appointees—must be working towards a common goal and doing so vigorously, ethically, respectfully, and with intense focus. This is the only way to push ahead on projects; it is a group effort in the truest sense, meaning it's imperative that all parties be aligned to the greatest degree possible.

But this in turn demands firm, committed leadership. The Executive Branch should be seen as a funnel that narrows at the top and widens at the bottom. At the very top is the president, and as his or her choices filter down, it falls upon those in the rungs below his or hers to lead the parties below them towards their goals.

Leaders must bring their teams together and focus their efforts on advancing the president's goals. In practice, this means that leaders must be informed, analytical, willing and able to explain their strategies, and in touch with their teams. Everything starts at the top. Leaders need to remember that fact and demonstrate it in their work.

The most important thing a leader can do aside from leading by example is making good personnel choices. This is because an organization is only as good as its weakest link. In the next chapter, we discuss the importance of personnel and team building. As we will see, this is a problem that has vexed Republicans for the entirety of the party's history.

CHAPTER 5

PERSONNEL IS POLICY

You Get What You Vote for—Sometimes

Journalists and political scientists love to complain about the American political system for a variety of reasons, most of them relating to the Separation of Powers and our unique republican form of government. You know, some of the few things in American politics that are actually good, and which mostly work.

Since Donald Trump beat the D.C. Establishment in 2016, much of their bellyaching has turned on the issue of voting. Specifically, their frustration is with our approach to voting: apparently, it's undesirable because it doesn't represent the full range of views held by the voting public, among other things. A different system, one that allows for ranked voting perhaps, is held up as preferable—never mind that such a system is unfeasible and tedious wherever it has been tried.[85]

But for the purposes of this book, I must concede that, much as I disagree with these progressives' objectives to further distort our voting system, these critics have a point in at least one regard: we do have a substantial issue with our elections, but only on the Republican side. That is, there has been and remains an enduring principal-agent problem between voters and their representatives. Stated bluntly, voters support a candidate who represents an issue or collection of issues but end up getting something very different once the candidate takes his or her office.

This dilemma is probably most true when it comes to the Executive Branch. But to be clear, this issue isn't caused by the selected representative of the people, i.e., the elected president. Rather, it is with *his* agent, in this case D.C. Republicans. And unfortunately, the cases of both President Trump and President Reagan highlight the issue.

Taking a step back, let's define this economics concept. The principal-agent problem is fundamentally a conflict in priorities between a person or group and the representative authorized to act on their behalf. While this sounds confusing, the idea is straightforward: person *A* gives certain responsibilities to person *B*, and person *B* has different plans for the responsibilities he or she has been given. A gap opens, and therein is the problem.

In my view, this issue is especially bad when it comes to hiring in the Executive Branch. Voters (the principal) select their candidate (the agent), and if he or she wins, then that person in turn delegates power to others (another agent or agents) to advance certain goals. This arrangement is inescapable due to the simple fact that presidents are far too busy to be involved in the selection process for their many subordinates. Indeed, it's unlikely that a president can or would pick out his or her entire cabinet. Plus, voters can't possibly vote for personnel; it wouldn't make any sense and would be incredibly inefficient and unworkable if attempted.

The upshot is that elected presidents must, during the transition period from November to January, delegate some degree of authority on many of the most important structural tasks related to the staffing of the Executive Branch. The challenge that presidents face is this: How much authority should they delegate, and on what issues should they remain the final decision-maker?

Ultimately, I firmly believe that presidents shouldn't turn over the entire hiring process to anyone—especially not their VPs—because of the principal-agent and its potential risks. Typically, presidents will make certain high-level or critical selections (e.g., Attorney General or Chief of Staff) themselves and then turn the remaining selection process over to their staff, often under the direction of their VPs.

As we will see below, this seemingly straightforward task of staffing the remainder of the Executive Branch has led to headaches, setbacks, and in the worst cases, the undermining of entire presidencies. And at the end of the chapter, I will outline a safer, more reliable alternative to VP-driven delegation of staffing responsibilities.

VP Disloyalty

As referenced above, Presidents Trump and Reagan encountered the principal-agent dilemma when they turned over the responsibility of staffing their administrations to their subordinates (Mike Pence and George H. W. Bush, respectively). Voters liked Trump and Reagan, and they especially liked the *central* issues they ran on (immigration, closing left-wing agencies, etc.). What they got in terms of policy once both men were sworn in, however, was not exactly what was advertised. Regrettably, in some crucial respects, it was much less.

To be clear, this is not really a problem with Reagan or Trump. They were both human, meaning that, as presidents, they could not engage in the time-consuming process of staffing their governments. On top of that, they were both political outsiders—a point that is especially crucial for understanding because of its significance on the options available before them re: staffing and hiring. Trump never even worked in government previously while Reagan's entire political operation was on the other side of the country. Both men ran against D.C. and the political Establishment residing there.

So, who *could* these conservative reformers count on to staff their governments? The difficulty is that, while both Trump and Reagan ran and won on being reformers, their vice presidents—the men who staffed their White Houses and much of the Executive Branch—were defenders of the *status quo*.

In fact, there is a strong argument to be made that both Pence and Bush were representative of the D.C. Establishment before anything else. I would go a step further and say that an objective assessment of the situation shows that both Pence and H. W. Bush were parts of the very swamp that their superiors sought to drain. Let's review both men in turn, starting with Pence.

Pence was a longtime congressman who was as conventional a D.C. Republican as any; he sometimes talked tough on issues near and dear to the hearts of base voters but just as quickly retreated when pressed.[86] Most recently, Pence was in the running for president, and his candidacy is tied to the outdated and unpopular D.C. Republican policy of stressing fiscal responsibility while at the same time talking out the other side of his mouth about the need to spend more on defense.[87]

More concerning was the fact that Pence, during the transition and as VP, got along with a lot of people who were vehemently opposed to President Trump—not only during the primaries, but also in the general election.[88] Having friends with opposing views is one thing; it is another altogether to hire them into key positions within an administration they actively opposed, particularly when doing so meant skipping over others who were all-in on then-candidate Trump.[89]

As for H. W. Bush, there isn't much to say beyond pointing out that his resume is probably the swampiest of any vice president, save for Joe Biden. For background, he was part of a Republican political dynasty, served in the military, was a multi-term former congressman, and career spook; and don't forget that he had a pretty liberal voting record during his first tour in D.C.[90] But the most conspicuous issue with Bush—and the one that suggested problems to come—is that he ran against Reagan in 1980 for the Republican Party's nomination, and did so from the Left.[91] Put simply, the ideological gap between the two was massive.

The upshot is that neither Mike Pence nor George H. W. Bush would rock the proverbial boat in the way that their respective presidents intended to and won on. To reiterate, in many important cases, this is because both men differed substantially from their bosses on key issues, e.g., Pence is and remains a champion of robust American intervention abroad[92] and is uncritical of the manifest problems with the military, while Bush infamously trashed Reagan's signature economic plan and took far more socially liberal positions than his boss.[93]

In some respects, these men were fine VP selections. Their tickets did win, after all. But they were failures in that they undermined the vital missions of their presidents when they were called on to staff the Executive Branch. Indeed, the crucial problem was giving them the power to make key personnel decisions for the administrations in which they served.

This is the Executive Branch's principal-agent problem in a nutshell: Pence and Bush were given staffing responsibilities by their respective superiors, and rather than advance the clearly articulated goals of their principals by hiring people who shared their visions on key policies, they elevated people who a reasonable person would assume would not further those objectives because of their expressed views on those same issues, not to mention the candidates themselves.

And no one should read this and think that these mistakes were incidental. Both Bush and Pence had political goals beyond being VP, meaning that, at some level, these subversive hiring decisions factored into their long-term objective of running for president. Another way to think about the hiring is that these men wanted to cultivate power and make allies who might, down the road, support them for president. Giving away ultra-desirable jobs at powerful agencies is a great way to further that end, especially when the cost is to their bosses rather than themselves.

This situation is grim, and I think it gives some context for why so many of President Trump's former appointees have turned on him and taken to TV and print to trash him: they never *really* worked for him in the first place, so they don't see this as any type of disloyalty. And sadly, I think they are correct on that score.

The Reagan Revolution That Wasn't

Ronald Reagan comfortably won two presidential elections in the 1980s. Though Republicans didn't have total control of the government during his tenure, he nonetheless arrived in Washington, D.C. with a mandate to govern that was expanded following the 1984 election. And what was that mandate? Based on his campaign, the issues that Reagan won on, to distill them to a few concrete topics, were the economy, foreign policy, and the budget.

In his first term, Reagan traded a balanced budget for a defense buildup.[94] In a perfect world, Reagan obviously would have radically cut social spending, but a Democratic majority in the Congress rendered that goal impossible. And so, he was forced to compromise. He determined that increasing military spending was the more important task.

Fast forward four years, and despite winning by a wider margin in 1984, Reagan was again unable to secure a balanced budget for the same reason as earlier. Most importantly, he failed to address the social and governmental issues that he made central to his reelection bid, among them shrinking the size of the Executive Branch, promoting social conservatism, and reducing the power of D.C. *writ large*.[95] Reagan had a good presidency, but it was not transformative in the long-term, at least not in the way some suggest. Seeing the roots of this failure is instructive.

Looking back, I think we idealize Reagan for what he represented and what he *hoped* to accomplish. This fond reflection is no doubt influenced by the fact that, by any standard, Reagan was one of the most personable, optimistic, calm, and pleasant presidents in American history. Consequently, we see in Reagan what we want to see.[96] What makes this upsetting is that those attributes could have helped to realize several of Reagan's goals that went unfulfilled. So, what happened?

In a handful of cases, the wrong people were put into critical roles, and when the moment arrived for them to take a particular action, they froze and failed. Probably the most infamous case of this relates to the failed attempt to shutter the Department of Education (DOE), which, contrary to what some say, has always been a bastion of progressive activism and social engineering.

Reagan's critics often derided him as dull and too old (something that seems quaint given Biden's mental problems today), but he was far shrewder than they realized. Indeed, his understanding of D.C. was extensive, and he saw clearly the threat inherent in agencies with lots of funding, a nebulous mandate, gameable rules, and assertive, ideological bureaucrats. DOE was his main target, which I think positively speaks to his instincts and political literacy given the many problems it continues to cause in 2023.[97]

In his first term, Reagan tapped Terrel Bell, a well-liked man with an extensive background in education who served Presidents Nixon and Ford. Somewhat swampy and not particularly combative, Bell backed down from Reagan's call to dismantle DOE when he was told that such action would require legislative approval. Rather than challenge the rule, Bell opted instead to study educational outcomes. (In D.C., "studying" an issue translates into not addressing the issue.) In short, he folded, and nothing happened for four years.

Given the dynamics of Reagan's White House, it's highly likely that Chief of Staff (CoS) James Baker played a role in Bell's hiring, as well as the decision to forgo any serious challenge to the determination that he could not undo DOE. For background, Baker was a genius as well as a supremely swampy D.C. Republican with long ties to the Bush family; he also famously opposed Reagan in '76 and '80.[98] It's clear that his elevation to CoS was Bush's doing, and in that influential role he promoted people and policies that broke with those that Reagan campaigned on and believed in.

But in term two, it looked like things might change. Bell retired in 1984 and Reagan won a huge electoral victory, meaning the conservative reformer was presented with a second chance to restructure (if not retire) the DOE. Instead of picking someone more ideologically aligned, he went with William Bennett, a registered Democrat who previously ran the powerful National Endowment for the Humanities (NEH), where he himself was a second option to the more conservative Mel Bradford, who was shot down by squishy Republicans and neoconservatives in and outside of the administration.[99]

The rejection of Bradford at NEH and the elevation of Bennett at DOE both have their genesis in the rising influence of those in the Reagan White House who were, to put it mildly, not aligned with the larger reform mission. What makes this a problem is that NEH is one of the most influential agencies dealing with education. It controls immense sums of money (almost $6 billion) and has the power to nudge educational institutions and to exert real influence over the academy via its funding powers.[100] Put bluntly, it had the power to pump the brakes on many of the worrying trends in education that were rising in the 1980s and which would become manifest in only a few short years—so much so that even liberals would take issue with it.[101]

But instead, Bennett issued a celebrated and worthless study on the teaching of the humanities in higher education.[102] He didn't use the full force of NEH when he ran the agency, and he didn't do anything aggressive at DOE at a time when it was beginning to abuse non-discrimination rules to meddle in the curricula and other policies of schools around the country.

The silver lining, however, is that when Bennet left the administration in 1988, he did so as a Republican (he finally switched his party after serving eight years for a Republican president). That is a small consolation for what amounted to a wasted term to fix DOE at the zenith of Reagan's political powers, which is to say nothing of the non-use of NEH's influence to shape a devolving educational situation in the US. Sarcasm aside, this eight-year stretch was an abject failure that left so much on the proverbial table, much of it of the low-hanging fruit variety. Tragically, few Republican presidents since have even expressed interest in returning to the proposed reforms to DOE that Reagan ran on.

It's normally useless to imagine a world where one or two small factors were changed. Nonetheless, I can't help but wonder how different things would have been had Bush not been selected VP, or if Baker hadn't been selected as CoS, or even if Reagan had simply outsourced hiring to someone loyal to his mission. We may never know what would have happened. But we do know that, in a very fatal way, the personnel decisions that Reagan delegated to Bush contributed to a missed opportunity to reform D.C. in a fundamental manner.

The Stolen Election of 2016

Now let's look at the more recent example of the Trump Administration. President Trump's main issue on the campaign trail was immigration, which was punctuated by his promises to enforce existing immigration laws on the one hand, and to build a wall that Mexico would pay for on the other. One would expect that the Executive Branch would be built around these signature goals.

As we know, this didn't happen. In fact, once Chris Christie was pushed out, it was Mike Pence, the man tasked with staffing, who brought in an array of people who didn't support President Trump's campaign for the White House, let alone the policies that he ran on to "Make America Great Again" during his tenure. Moreover, they did not attempt to hide this. Furthermore, many of these same people were not at all interested in taking meaningful action on immigration and immigration-related policies; others were unwilling to take on other prominent problems, including removing the DEI training racket from the federal government.

From my view, this decision by Pence was inexcusable. He was on the campaign trail with President Trump and heard what he intended to do in office; he even echoed the policies and promises that the MAGA agenda was centered on. He had been in politics long enough at that point to understand how the game works, and especially how serious the principal-agent problem can be in and around the public sector.

But beyond all that, Pence broke the cardinal rule of politics: help those who help you. The logic of the *quid pro quo*—something for something—is (or should be) at the heart of many personnel decisions. You should always help those who help you, both because it's the right thing to do but also because it signals that you value loyalty by practicing it in return. Many of President Trump's most ardent supporters were completely frozen out of the administration, and few ever got a chance to serve the president they did so much for when he was a candidate.

The bottom line is that Pence didn't care about the MAGA agenda, and that sad truth is underscored by the terrible personnel decisions he made in early 2017. Many of these issues have their roots in the poorly run Presidential Personnel Office (PPO) at the beginning of the Trump Administration.

An influential White House office can help to drive issues throughout an administration. Similarly, a badly run White House office can retard a president's efforts by failing to pressure agencies and the political appointees therein. Case in point: more terrible rules issued by President Obama's administration were allowed to hang around for years while Trump Administration attorneys dawdled and succeeded in avoiding their work.[103]

The Trump administration's failures in the hiring process during the early days was doubly bad because getting personnel right on the front end ensures greater coherence over the course of an administration. And the opposite is true, too: starting off poorly makes correcting the course much harder down the line, so to speak.

I concede that, in some cases, there are only a few candidates for a particular role, and perhaps none of the options is ideal. The reality of politics is that, to a high degree, the system is one defined by a revolving door through which only a relatively small number of individuals can pass through. Certain people will come and go; they enter government from conservative organizations and return when their time is up. Sadly, this arrangement oftentimes exacerbates the principal-agent issue detailed above.

It is for this very reason that getting hiring right is essential: sometimes it is the last defense against self-interested appointees who want to pursue their own goals and ignore those of the principal(s) they serve. Some of these people are necessary team-members, but they can never be leaders if (and when) their views break with those of the president. As with the funnel metaphor in the prior chapter re: presidential power, staffing an administration operates in the same way, i.e., with principals and leaders, before moving down.

If too many of these undesirable, non-aligned people are put into critical roles, then big policy goals with which they disagree will get sidelined or worse. To use a concrete example, there is a reason that the border wall was given a backseat to both the aborted attempt to repeal Obamacare and to the tax cuts: those in President Trump's White House, and indeed his cabinet,[104] were more amenable to the goals of Paul Ryan, Mitch McConnell, and the Chamber of Commerce than they were to President Trump and the voters who got him elected.[105]

In other words, the 2016 election of Donald Trump, made possible by the voters who believed in his message and wanted his policies enacted, was stolen. And it wasn't stolen by Russians, but by the Republicans whose candidates Trump summarily defeated in the Republican Primaries.

The Republican Establishment got much of what it wanted out of the Trump Presidency, including a host of policies that diverged radically from the policies Trump cared about, e.g., the passage of a jailbreak bill[106] that couldn't have been further from President Trump's expressed interest in executing drug dealers,[107] and the further institutionalization of NATO, of which Trump was (and remains) dubious.[108]

In sum, where the 2020 Election was stolen via illegal changes to election law, the effectiveness of the 2016 Election was hampered by a cadre of Never-Trump Republicans who whittled their way into key administrative positions, self-interested careerists, and swamp monsters who commandeered the presidency of a man they hated and never supported. Meanwhile, President Trump's voters were iced out of the administration and, unsurprisingly, many grew disillusioned with the MAGA movement and with the larger political system. This is reducible to bad personnel policy. It is unacceptable and cannot happen again.

In these final sections, we will review a few solutions to these personnel problems, including the important lessons that must guide decision-making in the next Republican administration. That discussion begins with a brief commentary on an important reality of public service that Republicans must wake up to.

It's the Incentives, Stupid

Something that I don't think many people understand, but which is essential for understanding the personnel problem, is the idea of appointees using their public service as a stepping stone for their careers. In theory, this is totally kosher. After all, working in the government expands one's understanding of the relationship between the state and the market, it teaches new skills, etc. In fact, in a perfect world, I believe that effective appointees *should* walk into new opportunities after they serve.

As with so many things concerning American politics, this isn't how it works in practice. Sure, those who work in Democrat administrations will get certain perks in hiring and in graduate school programs. One reason for this is because they're sure to throw money and other benefits at the education system. Conservatives are at least nominally trying to do the opposite. After all, reducing the power of D.C. necessarily means breaking up its various connections to universities and industries.

On top of that, we as conservatives are also trying to restrict bad policies that benefit these same institutions, such as affirmative action, and the many financial benefits they get in promoting DEI, social-engineering, etc. In short, we are opposed to many aspects of the corporate world as well as the academy, meaning we are unlikely to leave office with great offers from these same entities.

The upshot is that, if you do a good job as a Republican appointee in the Executive Branch, then you are not going to get a golden parachute from the rotten institutions you tried to reform during your tenure in office. In fact, there is a decent chance you'll get investigated and harassed after you leave office. (I will return to this in later chapters.)

What I saw from my perch at EPA is that many Republican appointees either did not understand that, or they did understand it and adjusted their behavior accordingly. The former is excusable while the latter is not. Recently hired appointees should know, but perhaps also should be told in the interview process, that their service may not benefit them financially or career-wise in the long-term. Being honest upfront about the mission and the expected results is only fair.

To address the second problem, I think a warning upfront would also go a long way. Those in the interviewing and hiring business could tell interviewees that, if you do a good job and, say, remove funds from left-wing organizations, or take on the race regime at DOJ or DOE, then there is a good likelihood that your previous employer—be it a white shoe law firm or a consulting agency—will not want you back. There is a thin membrane between the state and the market, and Democrats understand that and have taken steps to exert political control, meaning that effective conservative reformers will get treated unfairly if and when they return to the private sector.

If that isn't acceptable to interviewees, then that's fine. There's no issue. The problem only arises when they agree to serve and refuse to follow the president's orders to take on those types of entities. I know for a fact that several high-level appointees in the Trump Administration—some of them at the principal-level—refused to implement President Trump's September 2020 Executive Order on Combating Race and Sex Stereotyping. They preferred to violate the chain of command within the Executive Branch rather than instruct their agencies to take on these rackets for fear that doing so would hurt their private sector careers.[109]

In some cases, these principals were attorneys who understood that these actions were racist and illegal under existing civil rights law. No matter. They still wormed their way out of doing what was just, legal, and their job. That is a damning indictment of the quality of Republican appointees from the D.C. swamp; it's also a sad testament to the low-quality, worthless process that Pence and his subordinates used when making hiring decisions.

Making smart personnel decisions means taking these incentives into consideration and mitigating them when possible. In other cases, it includes using other incentives to get them to work for your agenda, not against your goals. A candid conversation with potential employees is a good starting point, because it is imperative that Republican appointees understand what they are getting themselves into.

Long-term, I think the problem of asymmetrical career tracks for former Schedule C political appointees can be resolved almost entirely by depoliticizing the private sector, which necessarily entails successfully taking on DEI, reining in the anti-discrimination complex, and instituting a true system of justice in America.

No doubt, these are massive goals that are only achievable through radical reform, which in turn requires sustained focus and deep resolve. As such, I will give these objectives greater space in the following chapters. To put a coda on the personnel discussion, let's discuss a few short institutional reforms to the hiring and staffing processes.

Recruitment and Institution-Building

In my view, I think the bigger picture reform movement is going to need to rely on institutions, those in existence now as well as new and nascent institutions. The common thread across these organizations will be, individually and in concert, to recruit, educate, and prepare future appointees and civil servants to effectively deal with what has, heretofore, been an enduring problem—namely, navigating the swamp, contending with the bureaucracy, and peeling back the rules and norms built up around the rival Constitution.

This is a big task, and it becomes infinitely more complex when one realizes that the full force of the media, bureaucracy, and progressive movement will fight any effort to remove political power from D.C. And that doesn't even begin to account for the fact that this project will be expensive and time sensitive.

Thankfully, the institution-building effort is not wholly ground up. The Heritage Foundation is an existing think tank that celebrated its fiftieth birthday earlier this year. It is tied into the conservative movement in America, and it has great scholars and a large budget. On top of that, during Democratic administrations, it undertakes the thankless task of preparing for the next Republican transition via its "transition projects." Right now, Heritage is working on preparing the next Republican administration for its transition period.

At the same time, other organizations are popping up to further prepare the next cohort of Republican appointees to enter the swamp. Hillsdale College's Van Andel Graduate School of Statesmanship teaches its students about the all-important first-principles of the American Constitution, which are critical to keep in mind as we seek to restore the charter for our system of government.

More recently, other entities have set out with even narrower missions. For instance, American Moment is a conservative organization that specializes in personnel. Its explicit goal is to "identify, educate, and credential young Americans who will implement public policy . . ." to serve in the Executive Branch and elsewhere.[110] By connecting students and young professionals to more established and experienced conservative activists, civil servants, and experts, American Moment seeks to impart on its fellows key lessons about the institutional challenges they will likely face when they serve in the next Republican Administration.

There are a host of other organizations that deserve mention, but to give all of them their due would be a task beyond the space allowed in this chapter. Ultimately, the main point here is that organizations are explicitly working to better prepare Republicans for their next crack at running the federal government. This is a great development, but that is only half the metaphorical battle.

The other issue to address is recruitment. As mentioned earlier, there are only so many choices available to Republicans when it comes to staffing. The reasons are numerous. For instance, many qualified people don't want to move to D.C.; some don't want to give up their current job to make less money in the public sector; professionals worry the affiliation with a Republican administration could close doors to them; and others are doers who understand that working in the government as a conservative necessarily entails frustration and could well amount to no tangible successes.

These are all valid points, but in truth, there is still far more that Republicans who want to change D.C. can do to bring in talented individuals who will add value to teams across the Executive Branch. Organizations like the Federalist Society were essential in locating and assembling talented, mostly like-minded attorneys who, years later, went on to help staff the Judiciary and the Executive Branch. Creating similar organizations in the business world and in the medical field would be two ways of creating networks into those professions that could in turn be counted on to help staff certain positions at the Departments of Labor, Health and Human Services, and Treasury, to use a few examples.

This is not an immediate fix, but it's a systematic approach that is worth investing in. Given the amount of questionably spent money floating around in the world of Republican politics, putting some of it towards this project could go a long way in boosting the talent available to future Republican presidents.

In closing, the personnel issue is an enormous and critically important one. While it was not a good thing that the issue became so prominent in recent years, we owe President Trump thanks for highlighting how bad things had become. Similarly, it was President Trump who again made reform—draining the swamp, breaking the juggernaut that is D.C.—central to his platform, and to the broader Republican agenda.

Bringing consequences to D.C. is essential—for the federal bureaucracy and to the Republican Party. In the next chapter, we will discuss the uglier sides of recent D.C. history, namely the failures of Republicans to impact enduring change in the DMV. Later, we will review some more positive lessons, as well as future plans to upend the *status quo*.

CHAPTER 6

PAST FAILURES: REFLECTIONS & LESSONS

Not Negative—Nuanced

The last few chapters have not been the most uplifting. From explaining why many federal employees should be fired to detailing the ways in which conservative voters get hoodwinked after the candidates they support win their races, the content as of late has trended more negative than positive. If you read the last dozen pages and came away defeated, then rest assured: things will get better from here.

As I said early on, I'm an upbeat person, and I didn't write this book to make the reader feel dejected or angry. Rather, I wrote it to give an honest account of where we as conservatives are with respect to realizing our goal of reforming D.C. by draining the swamp. Honesty demands that I give a true assessment of where things stand, and right now, they aren't great. We have an immense challenge before us that, for too long, our representatives ignored; and when we took it seriously, we didn't approach it as best we could.

In this chapter, we will review some of the conservative movement's failings—not to wallow in defeat or to imagine how different our world would be today if we had succeeded in the past, but to learn from our errors. I firmly believe that no mistake is fatal in politics; there will always be a second chance because voters are human, meaning they can and likely will change their minds on an array of different issues and events. By learning, we prepare and improve.

As such, my goal for this chapter is to lay out some of those mistakes to divine lessons from them. These lessons in turn can and will inform some of the decisions we make and the strategies we employ when we get that next opportunity to reform the government in D.C. Seeing this larger political project in this light—i.e., as a long journey across many election cycles rather than a quick battle after a single election—is essential if we are to approach the issue in an intelligible and effective manner.

Turning to that next section, I think that the best place to begin is with an especially painful defeat, one that conservatives dealt with for decades and which, at many times, felt utterly hopeless. The logic in doing so is that we will see just how great the payoff was, as well as the critical strategic adjustments that were made to succeed in the effort to reform the first major institution to be captured by progressives: the Supreme Court.

The 50 Year Fight for the Supreme Court

Having spent so much time in Republican politics, I can attest to the pervasive feelings of frustration and defeat within our coalition—some of which even accompanied electoral victories. I try to be a positive person, but I'm also a realist, so I understand that many of my fellow conservatives have a rationally negative outlook on the political situation in America, particularly in D.C.

In my experience, much of this pessimism is rooted in the fact that, for many election cycles, Republicans would win at the ballot box (sometimes decisively), and then, only a few years later, would have nothing to show their voters. And at the same time, public opinion and most major institutions in America would move further to the left on social issues. In short, it felt like our wins at the federal level meant nothing. We had no tangible results, and at the same time, the country slouched even further towards the embrace of progressive values.

When I tried to understand the development of this attitude, which seemed to peak when conservative power was waxing (or at least had not yet begun to wane), I was at a bit of a loss. Sure, by the 2000s Republicans were struggling to win the popular vote nationwide, but we were nonetheless making huge strides in the states on a host of critical issues, from education reform[111] to breaking union power and even tallying wins on abortion.[112] So, what was the genesis of all this negativity and hopelessness?

It was only by looking back at the larger history of conservative politics in America that I began to get a sense for this broad, enduring negativity. The New Deal Constitutional Revolution was one of the lowest points for conservatives in America. It marked the end of the rule of the Founders' Constitution; our constitutional system was turned on its head, and we remain far away from setting it straight some eighty years later. This was a terrible turn, but I don't think this was the event that led to a kind of sad fatalism in Republican politics.

On the contrary, I think that we need to return for a moment to Reagan's presidency. The quintessential "happy warrior," Reagan inspired in his followers a sense of national pride, and a belief that anything was possible. As mentioned in the previous chapter, some of this optimism was undue, in part because the actual Reagan legacy is far more mixed than many want to admit. At the same time, however, I think that the one element of Reagan's tenure that many Republicans now openly admit was a disaster was his selection of Supreme Court nominations, two of whom infamously upheld and expanded the logic of Warren Court liberalism that the president promised to reverse.[113]

Before we can talk about Reagan's judicial selections and their impact, it's necessary to say a word about the Judicial Branch, and that means looking at the 1930s again. This is because it was in this period that the constitutional order was overturned, and that proved a transformative development for the judiciary, much to the chagrin of conservatives.

The New Deal Constitutional Revolution transformed the "least dangerous branch" into the most powerful, sweeping, and unaccountable branch—a somewhat ironic development given that FDR's New Deal judges were originally proponents of judicial restraint.[114]

The next generation was far less modest in the use of its power. Indeed, the Supreme Court could make laws as it saw fit and restructure society and political systems, and it did so under Chief Justice Warren's direction, with little concern for the country's legal tradition, let alone the popular sentiments in American society.[115]

As all this was going on, the other branches had no meaningful recourse. The Supreme Court is, after all, the final arbiter on the Constitution. Under the Warren Court, however, the Constitution was not enough; the Left had to transform the Court into the final arbiter of American culture.

The nadir (or high point, depending on one's politics) was probably the infamous and now reversed *Roe v. Wade* decision, which invented a right to abortion absent any substantive textual basis.[116] (While this case technically occurred *after* the Warren Era ended, it was brought about by and consistent with the legal theories of Warren's court.) The case set abortion policy across the country, overturning scores of popularly enacted laws in the process. In many respects, this was the catalyst for the formation of the conservative legal movement. But I would caution against seeing the conservative legal movement as a mere reaction to one especially bad case.

Whether Republicans took issue with the specific policy outcomes of the Warren Court was secondary to their main critique, which turned on the issue of institutional degradation. As they rightly saw it, the bigger issue was that the Supreme Court was violating the all-important principle of the Separation of Powers; it was effectively stealing from the Legislature the prerogative to make laws, a usurpation that damaged both branches. This transgression was unacceptable and had to stop. As such, Republicans committed themselves to restoring the old constitutional order, and the Judicial Branch's proper place therein.

The excesses of the Warren Court were a political boon for Republicans: it helped them to win a handful of presidential elections, starting in 1968 when the explicitly anti-Warren Court campaign of George Wallace split the Democrats.[117] Nixon, Reagan, etc.—all the Republican candidates (many of them successful)— ran on reining in the Supreme Court and mitigating the disasters it wrought in civil society, e.g., the explosion of crime in the 1960s and 1970s.[118]

Of course, to effectively rein in the Supreme Court, Republican presidents would need to nominate judges loyal to and intent on restoring the original Constitution, and the Senate would need to confirm them. This is where things got difficult: Republican presidents in this period had a pathetic record of nominating truly conservative judges, and Reagan's record was especially bad.

From Nixon to H. W. Bush, Republicans only nominated and got confirmed a few good judges to the High Court, none of them totally perfect. Among the mostly good to great judicial nominations were Scalia, Rehnquist, and Thomas. At the same time, they put forth and got confirmed a handful of awful judges, including but not limited to Stevens, Kennedy, O'Connor, Blackmun, and Souter. And many other judges they nominated moved to the left, so it is not as though the other selections were that much better than the most egregious selections.

Put simply, Republican presidents nominated to the Supreme Court *at least* as many progressives as they did conservatives from roughly 1969 through 1992. Nixon and H. W. Bush, who had shorter terms in office, each put forth and had confirmed one excellent pick, Rehnquist and Thomas, respectively. But to be fair, Nixon had the most nominations (four total) and only made one great selection. And don't forget Ford, whose lone Supreme Court nomination—John Paul Stevens—was as bad a mistake as any.[119]

Reagan had the longest term in office of any president between 1968 and 1992. Moreover, he also had three (or four, depending on how one counts) chances to change the court for the better. Reagan's only good original contribution was Scalia, whose influence on the conservative legal movement remains immense today. (Reagan also nominated Rehnquist to the position of Chief Justice, which was an admittedly great move.) But his other picks were very bad; Kennedy and O'Connor were failures, and the Bork and Ginsburg fiascos were badly mismanaged.

The results speak for themselves: Republicans failed for more than fifty years to restore the Supreme Court to an at least neutral institution. That failure was made worse by the fact that they nominated the majority of the Supreme Court Justices over that period, and over half were hard left in their judicial philosophy. Fast forward to the present day, and the Court is no longer a left-wing institution. Indeed, winning back the Supreme Court is one of President Trump's greatest achievements, and the culmination of a decades-long effort that required genuine political bravery from the ordinarily pusillanimous Republicans in the Senate.

But make no mistake, the effort to save the Supreme Court took generations to achieve. Moreover, organizations such as the Federalist Society as well as effective political action committees (PACs) were invaluable. Indeed, it was a recognition that the task would take years combined with the ingenuity and effort of trained professionals that finally allowed reformers to return a majority that takes the Constitution seriously to the High Court.

If any other efforts at addressing the rot in D.C. are to be successful, then they must be similarly focused, funded, fearless, and realistic about the scope of the problem before them. Sometimes the only way to win in politics is to make tough decisions that hurt you in the short-term. Few lasting victories are won overnight.

Unsurprisingly, progressives have become apoplectic on all things related to federal courts. They attack the Supreme Court all the time now, and it's clear that there is a deep bitterness about losing the first institution in D.C. that they captured.[120] Republicans must be prepared for efforts to attack the High Court now that it is no longer a tool at the disposal of progressives.

Critically, the fifty-year Supreme Court saga offers a key lesson: reform in D.C.—even the most well-planned, well-funded, and agreed-upon reform effort within the conservative movement—can take *decades* to bring about. And if it succeeds, then prepare for serious blowback. As we review some of the reasons as to why we have failed to drain the swamp, please keep this central lesson in mind.

The Glamour Factor

In a world in which attention spans are declining, it can be a challenge to keep oneself engaged with a task. Distractions are everywhere, and I can personally attest to the reality that we as people prefer to do things that are attainable in the short-term. Moreover, we prefer to pursue goals that are exciting, attention-getting, and have discernable metrics for success, like beating a level in a video game or completing an assignment for work or school.

Another way of looking at this truth is this: It's hard for people to get excited for—let alone to complete—work, projects, etc. that aren't glamorous, timely, or cool. As it happens, draining the swamp falls firmly into this category of projects.

Draining the swamp is not a single task, nor is it a problem that can be resolved cleanly in one year, or even one presidency. As mentioned earlier, this is because the formation of the swamp itself was a process of degradation that took decades to complete. Dredging it will be an immense task.

What makes this endeavor even more challenging is that it's a long-term project with many, many participants who must act in concert (to varying degrees) to make an impact. That some of these challenges require collective action across branches of government makes the situation even more challenging to coordinate and commit to.

Plus, when one encounters a roadblock, they usually just give up. This is exactly what happened with Reagan and his aborted attempt to end the Department of Education.[121] He and his team encountered pushback and dropped the issue altogether. Since then, no Republican president has seriously argued that the department needs to go.

But I want to talk about another factor. Specifically, the added difficulty is that there are far easier things to do that require less work and which are sure to garner more attention in the press. I'm not saying that political appointees don't want to make a difference; I am also not saying that pursuing other tasks—less difficult to achieve ones, for instance—is necessarily a bad thing.

What *I am saying*, and what I want to be clear about, is that, in a political world governed by limited windows to act, among other constraints, opting for one goal over another is a trade-off. Getting a feature in the press, whether negative or positive, can be a powerful and attractive incentive that does push appointees towards certain issues and away from others.

There is nothing sexy about breaking up power in D.C., in large part because this isn't simply an action that can be executed in one act, one term, or even one presidency. Likely, this will take decades of work *à la* restoring the Supreme Court. Again, I think that we, as Republicans, need to be candid about this reality, because there are reasons to think that many appointees may not be interested in participating in this admittedly dull, distant work.

Another reason why this work isn't glamorous is because, if you're serious about draining the swamp, then that means going up against D.C.'s biggest industries which are often golden parachutes for former appointees, Republican and Democrat like: lobbying and contracting. Working as a lobbyist or contractor in D.C. is extremely lucrative and hence very attractive. We've talked a bit about the revolving door side of politics, and nowhere is this more pronounced than in the worlds of lobbying and contracting. Representing a client's interests or securing a federal project can translate into big bucks for an attorney or consultant. Now imagine you can do the same without getting an expensive law degree or a certification.

This is lobbying, and depending on the client, industry, and ask (i.e., what the client wants you to do), you can make a lot of money for very little work. On top of that, actual knowledge and professional standards are not requirements. Just see the ongoing Hunter Biden saga for further proof.[122]

This is another element of draining the swamp that is unattractive: taking the project seriously means opposing lobbying and federal slush funds where you can, and likely taking yourself out of the revolving door system when you leave the administration. This is a potentially massive trade-off, and the only reward is knowing that your decision to forgo lobbying and/or contracting is going towards the greater good—but only if others do the same.

The prisoner's dilemma, another economic concept, is very much at play here.[123] Essentially, people need to coordinate to advance a goal that will leave them both better off. The problem is that they need to take the same action at the same time. If one or both breaks, then they are worse off. If one Republican appointee sells out and becomes a lobbyist, then everyone is worse off as the system is better able to perpetuate itself.

When I think about hiring and personnel, this problem gets much bigger and messier, particularly against the backdrop of draining the swamp. To put it bluntly, it may well be too much to ask of potential appointees to get them to promise not to lobby after their tenure in a Republican administration. In fact, I think the only way to *really* address this problem (to the extent it can be addressed at all) is to try to ban and/or limit lobbying by Executive Order or by statute. I won't hold my breath on the latter, but the former is at least a start.

The bigger picture problem is this: The entire incentive structure of D.C. is perverse. It rewards bad behavior, antisocial career choices, and in doing so serves to mitigate threats to its power, prestige, and centrality in American political life. I've sort of touched on this in this chapter and in previous chapters, but wanted to hold off on a direct discussion until we covered the necessary and adjacent topics.

The reason that the swamp has not been drained to this point is because it's a great deal for those in and around it. Personnel matters, and so does leadership. But outside of and alongside those issues is this much bigger, all-encompassing incentive dilemma. A central reason for that is that they don't bear the costs of this mess—but you, the everyday Americans outside D.C., do.

Swamp v. America

Sometimes, when I'm listening to a conservative radio show, the host will critique something crazy a journalist has written about why conservatives hate the government in D.C. Typically, the host presents an argument that seeks to explain the biased framing. Usually, the thesis is something like this: the journalist is just another Democrat hack who wants to push responsibility off liberals and progressives by blaming the victim, i.e., the Republican or independent voter.

In other words, the reason that journalists are so quick to condemn Republicans for hating the things Democrats do is simply to protect the latter politically. At one level, this is probably right, or at least not untrue. But in another sense, I think it misses the more direct explanation, or at least the one that we should focus on most, namely that the journalist lives in a bubble and thus doesn't understand why people are understandably and justifiably mad at progressives and their terrible policies.

And to clarify, this is not just any bubble. This is the bubble of all bubbles. The wealthy progressives in and around D.C. and other affluent cities (you know, the people living in the richest counties in the country) are totally blind to the awful impact they have on others via the policies and politicians they support and enable; and even when they trash their own cities, they have the wealth to sequester themselves off from the worst of the chaos.[124] The upshot is that they truly have no idea how destructive the policies are that they write about and defend, or they at least can remove themselves from the immediate vicinity and in turn the ugly process of reflection re: their own culpability.

In substantive terms, think about it like this. If you write for the *New York Times* or *Atlantic*, and you're trying to explain why voters outside of D.C. and off the coasts are mad about some crazy policy D.C. is pushing that they never voted on, odds are you'll never actually understand the reasons for their anger. The D.C. metro area is incredibly wealthy. Again, it's the richest part of the US, which may have something to do with the lobbying industry, the regulatory industry, et al. being largely situated in the nation's capital.[125]

When you have that much money, regulatory costs are diminished; when you have that much money, you can avoid crime via private security or a gated community; the list goes on and on. In short, you don't feel policies the way others do. So, if your policies are awful but you don't feel them, then why change course?

To clarify, I don't say that progressives in these wealthy areas are ignorant because of who they are; I don't think identity is the end-all, be-all for understanding others—I don't believe that for a second. No, I think this is the case because people in these bubbles are totally insulated from their policies because of their affluence. Classics scholar Victor Davis Hanson has written about this at length, and his essays should be read for a complete understanding of this issue.[126]

In any event, the main point is this: what progressives vote for in city elections, the Executive Branch policies they defend in academic papers, op-eds, etc.—they will never be touched by them. The D.C. swamp especially is an enclave for the reasons set out above. This is the reason why I see the issue of the swamp as being a dichotomy: it's D.C. (and those who benefit from living there and in its related coastal enclaves, e.g., NYC or San Francisco) vs. the rest of the country, i.e., the people who in no way shape, or form, consent to its radical, onerous edicts. The asymmetry in costs and benefits is a disaster that must be rectified.

And trust me, the rest of the country *really* feels those policies. Regulatory costs are immense under Democrat presidents, and they're always growing. Just look at the actions of the Biden Administration's EPA to see how impactful and untenable these actions are.

Biden's EPA has reversed every major reform by the Trump Administration that sought to benefit consumers. The worst of these was its decision to ban hydraulic fracking, which, in doing so, jeopardizes so many American interests, from viable energy costs to national security concerns. (Let the record reflect that the US was energy-independent under President Trump.)

But don't listen to me. Instead, check out a 2021 report from the Department of Energy; the paper highlighted all these problems—problems that are compounded by the fact that, at the same time, the Biden administration was pushing other rules to further hike the price of energy.[127] The sad and scary thing about this situation is that it was entirely self-inflicted. Democrats don't care and won't change course, in part because they are untouched by their choices.

Some of the other insane decisions by Biden & Co. include a host of bans on various energy and energy-related projects. These senseless bans hurt small businesses and American consumers, especially those Americans who live and work in the heartland. Energy costs in America are rising to unsustainable highs.[128] All the while, the Biden Administration continues to promulgate new rules to retard growth and add additional costs on energy producers that—as is always the case—get passed down to consumers.

Something is deeply wrong when Americans are paying more for their energy than countries with a fraction of the technology and natural resources that we have. Moreover, when we use these assets, the costs for consumers diminish and our national security interests are enhanced. But progressives don't care, so the prices won't be coming down anytime soon. The same holds true for crime and any other major problem in American life today. It doesn't hurt them, so why change course?

The Administrative State and its Deep State agencies and bureaucrats are broadly opposed to the interests of Americans outside the coasts, and to attempts at reform in particular. This is an unreasonable alliance predicated on ideology, meaning that no amount of debate or persuasion will have any impact. These actors and their institutions are not democratic; they are not influenced one way or another by elections. Reformers need to understand that and act accordingly, because the standard approaches don't work and never will.

Taking Ike Seriously

Reliving the disappointments of the past is never fun, and I promise that the remainder of the book is much more hopeful and positive. It's also more forward-looking, as we look to future solutions rather than dwell on dated failures. That said, there is one more conservative failure that must be touched on, because it is extremely instructive and vital. Specifically, that has been the contributions conservatives have made to the unchecked expansion of the military—an institution that is obsequious to progressives and rapacious in its efforts to get ever more money and influence in D.C.

At the end of President Eisenhower's term in office, he looked back on his tenure and the trajectory of the country. There was a lot he was proud of, but he also had serious concerns about the future of American life, as he saw the Cold War as ushering in worrisome changes in domestic society and politics that would destroy the internal "balance" necessary for a healthy system of democratic rule.

Though Eisenhower doesn't get much credit for it today, at least insofar as he's overshadowed by other Republican presidents, Ike was a committed conservative who understood that the threats facing the country were more than just foreign competitors. For that reason alone, I think conservatives ought to give Ike's wisdom a bit more consideration.

Turning to the text, Eisenhower's farewell address is read in schools and has been cited favorably by libertarians and liberals. Nowadays, I think progressives would reject his message given their support for the surveillance state and rent-seeking institutions in and around D.C. As such, conservatives should study Ike's remarks. The crux of the speech is that the "military-industrial complex" and the many institutions and practices built up around it are a necessary evil (emphasis on evil) that must be constrained and subject to intense scrutiny.

Eisenhower was terrified about what the growth of the military during peacetime would mean for American politics, our democracy, and our civil rights. As a military man, he understood that there are certain ideological undercurrents inherent in and inseparable from the military that make it, at least on some level, in conflict with civil society.[129]

Decades later, we see that Eisenhower was onto something. The line between domestic politics and the military is totally blurred in 2024; the increasing partisan involvement of military officers, retired and active, sounding off on political disputes[130] is unacceptable and as of today remains unchecked, despite the fact it flagrantly violates the Uniform Code of Military Justice and is sanctionable under the statute.[131] And then there is the issue of the revolving door between the military, government contractors, and high-ranking jobs within the Executive Branch. If D.C. is a swamp, then this convergence between the military and politics is a cesspool.

As it concerns draining the swamp, I think two lines from Eisenhower's remarks are especially important: "The potential for the disastrous rise of misplaced power exists and will persist. . . .

We must never let the weight of this combination endanger our liberties or democratic processes."

Unfortunately, what Eisenhower feared—the ascent and establishment of the military as a powerful, self-interested institution in American life—has come to pass. The most dramatic and scary truth of this is seen in the case of President Nixon, who challenged the power of the Pentagon to prosecute the Vietnam War: in reaction, the Joint Chiefs of Staff spied on the sitting president.[132] This was in the early 1970s, and as we know, the military has become bolder and more lawless since.[133]

But as is the case with pretty much all left-wing politics and institutions in the US, this is not because of a democratic vote or anything like that. Instead, it's been simple parasitism, and conservative disinterest with uprooting it.

Spelled out explicitly, the military—like the DEI racket, the environmentalist movement, left-wing curricula in public schools, the civil rights movement, etc.—is subsidized by the state. Its power was created by public money, secured through a mix of lobbying, media marketing, and disinterest by its critics and skeptics.

Have conservatives dropped the proverbial ball in allowing all these problems to grow unchecked? Of course. But the good news is that what they have signed off on in the past need not be sanctioned indefinitely into the future. In other words, reformers in D.C. have a lot of tools at their disposal to turn off the funds for these organizations, and in doing so can exert substantial influence over their actions and partisanship. Granted, much of this is in the hands of Congress, which is unlikely to touch the military for a variety of reasons. But a reform-minded president can do a lot to solve the problem on their own.

Furthermore, if we keep Eisenhower's wisdom in mind, we can look back and see the roadmap for taking apart entities like the military that have grown fat, smug, and unaccountable via enormous transfers of public funds and little to no oversight.

I think looking back at Eisenhower's warning is an excellent way to see how this problem of D.C.'s growth evolved, and in turn, how to begin to pair it back along with the institutions it has empowered and relies on for funds and protection against inquiries.

With that review complete, we have seen many of the failures of Republican presidents and well-meaning reformers. In the final chapters of the book, we will look ahead to the exciting but daunting work necessary to finally take on the Administrative State and to restore the proper balance of political power set out under the Constitution.

CHAPTER 7

A NEW CONSERVATIVE PROGRAM

The First Steps to Reform

As I have mentioned throughout the book, and what is hopefully clear by now, is that if any serious effort to reform D.C. is to be successful, then there must be a plan that: 1) envisions a clear, overarching goal; and 2) accounts for certain realities and factors, from personnel to mitigating adverse incentives, that must be considered if that goal is to be meaningfully pursued, let alone achieved. Historically, the failures of the conservative movement to address the many problems stemming from D.C. have turned on these two related issues.

At the beginning of the book, I said that, if we are to have any success in this great task, then it will be dependent on the formulation of a good plan. As demonstrated in previous chapters (especially Chapter 6), previous attempts to fix D.C. have been ill-thought out, loosely adhered to, and often forgotten or abandoned entirely when presented with the slightest pushback by progressives, be it in the bureaucracy or the media. Given the severity of time constraints and the limits of political choices, these errors have often been decisive in stifling reform efforts.

Thankfully, the organizational stage is already underway for a comprehensive plan to orient appointees—from principals and decision-makers down to lower-level team members—towards real, impactful, and attainable goals that will contribute to the broader, more expansive end of draining the swamp. And unlike in the past, this effort is more substantive, shared, and forward-looking than ever before.

Specifically, this project—an effort to better prepare for the next transition in the Executive Branch following Biden's defeat in November 2024—is being directed by the Heritage Foundation. For those who don't know, Heritage has undergone a transformation since President Trump's term in office and is all in on draining the swamp: the old, passive leadership was replaced with a new more dynamic core.[134] Its reform-focused enterprise is being oriented towards substantive results rather than boilerplate slogans, which regrettably have been the norm in Republican politics for decades.

Heritage's Project 2025 distinguishes itself from previous efforts in several important respects.[135] First, the effort is bringing in conservatives rather than boxing them out. This may sound ridiculous, but in the past, there were deliberate efforts by D.C. insiders to keep reformers away from certain roles and departments in Republican governments for fear that, if allowed in, they would take seriously the campaign promises to cut spending, shutter agencies, and root out partisans. In other cases, conservatives were not hired at all. But this time around, conservatives are steering the proverbial ship.

Second, Project 2025 has partnered with other conservative organizations and activists to help with the staffing and preparation side of the next Republican administration. In the past, this process was far too informal. Sure, Heritage would help to assemble policy books; it might make recommendations on individuals for certain roles. But there was far too much vagary, which as we saw in previous chapters, creates problems when presidents are forced to delegate authority to underlings, especially in staffing and hiring. All too often, swampy Republicans filled the gaps with bad appointees who didn't want to challenge the *status quo* in D.C.

By bringing in and working with partner organizations and conservative activists, Heritage is guaranteeing that the metaphorical bench for the next administration to draw on will be bigger and the personnel better informed on the issues, as well as more trained on navigating the rules and processes that the Deep State's allies hide behind. Additionally, there will also be more direction for those who are delegated hiring responsibilities, among other things.

The other added benefit of this approach is that it throws a wrench in the revolving door between conservative policy "experts," the think tanks they occupy between administrations, and high-ranking government roles they receive after elections. Hiring in future Republican administrations will be more meritocratic, with an emphasis on ability and ideology around certain goals or programs rather than preexisting relationships and proximity to longtime Republican fixtures in D.C. Appointees will be tasked with advancing team goals rather than simply sitting in offices while others work on their own self-interest assignments.

Finally, Project 2025 is undertaking the difficult but essential work of *preparing* appointees to govern. Set out in the *Mandate for Leadership* book, the Heritage Foundation and its aligned partner organizations outline numerous policies and programs that the next Republican administration should aggressively push on Day One. The book is exhaustive, with plans for each department, including advice that principals can utilize when they assume leadership roles.

Furthermore, *Mandate for Leadership* doubles as a technical resource for appointees. Have questions about a specific issue? Refer to the book. Want additional information about a metric for success re: a certain policy? Refer to the book. Unsure about how your role ties into the larger mission of the department? Need a reminder on the *mission* of your department? Refer to the book. And even if the book itself does not have answers, it will provide future appointees with a network to draw on and refer to when presented with a challenge in the Executive Branch.

In short, Heritage and its allies are building out a framework for governing unlike anything reformers have ever even imagined before. The basic idea is to position our people to not only begin on the right foot, but to have the capacity and wherewithal to make a difference that in turn positions us for greater success over time. Governing is more an art than a science, and any art must be honed and refined with time and experience. This is a comprehensive and excellent first step. Set out as a guide, we will look next at the second step.

But before going further into the discussion, I would be remiss not to mention the other efforts at institutionalizing a professional bench of future Republican appointees. Various organizations are devoting resources and thought to the personnel problem, including growth, development, and training, e.g., American Moment and the American First Policy Institute (AFPI). Taken together, these organizations are doing the hard but necessary work to position the next administration to govern, be it with recruitment or training. If there is one big takeaway from President Trump's first term, it is that a presidential agenda is only as good as the weakest link that contributes to its enactment. We will have better people in the next conservative administration to make sure that the variance between good appointees and great appointees is smaller than ever before.

The Ascendant Conservative Ideology

The second step for success that all reformers must recognize and adhere to is on the ideological side. Planning is important, but it is imperative that we have a clear and unifying understanding of what it is that we want to achieve in the next administration. The grassroots are invaluable, but at a practical level, governing is more top-down in terms of setting goals and executing them.

As of the writing of this section, the 2024 Republican Presidential Primaries are already over, with President Trump the decisive winner. While the former and future president did not participate in the various debates, he crushed the primaries. But even in President Trump's absence during the debates, the primaries were significant because they provided a means of looking into the future at the coming Republican agenda. While I will discuss the primaries in greater detail later in the book, for now, I want to talk a bit about why they are such a hopeful indicator of what is to come in future Republican-led governments.

First, there was a consensus across the leading candidates—President Trump, Governor Ron DeSantis, and billionaire businessman Vivek Ramaswamy—that the *status quo* in Washington, D.C. is untenable and must change. All three candidates acknowledged that the basic gears of government (the bureaucracy in particular) are one-sided, out of reach, and corrupt. The political institutions in D.C. are an impediment to reform, not a means to that end. Consequently, each candidate has at one point or another promised to fire partisans and shrink the size of the government workforce (an oxymoron), among other solutions.[136] (Those possible solutions will get full coverage later.) The rising ideological tide in the GOP is one of reform.

While it might be tempting to read these types of statements from the candidates and respond, "duh, of course the bureaucracy is progressive," I think it is worth mentioning that D.C. has had manifest issues for *decades* that Republican candidates—indeed *the conservative Republican candidates in presidential primaries*—have been unwilling or afraid to discuss.

I know it has been a long time, but try to think back to 2012. Back then, the frontrunner was Mitt Romney, the then former governor of Massachusetts, who was as squishy as ever. Romney was attacked as an *immigration hawk* for saying that he wanted illegal immigrants to "self-deport."[137] In contrast, Mr. Ramaswamy told the audience and the viewers on prime time television that Biden and Co. want to encourage illegal entry to get votes and dependents on the state as an electoral strategy.[138] Across the board, the leading Republicans are genuine hawks on immigration who want to finally solve the problem with a wall; others have talked about ending birthright citizenship.[139]

Elsewhere, these candidates agreed that basic institutions in America are broken, from the press to the military and the justice system. Governor DeSantis, to use one example, supported Senator Tuberville's "holds" on military promotions to protest efforts by the Biden Administration to break federal law by paying military service members to cover their costs for abortions.[140] Republicans must be willing to be aggressive with progressives when they violate the law, and they must also be open to breaking with some of the rent-seekers and bureaucracies that have been historically friendly to the GOP, e.g., the Pentagon.

To be sure, not all Republican candidates shared that view (Nikki Haley, Mike Pence, and Chris Christie were far less willing to speak candidly about institutional rot in America; depending on the issue, they denied it outright).[141] But the good news is that the other candidates did understand the nature of the problem. And the first step to solving a problem is admitting that there is a problem.

And the candidates were willing to name a variety of problems, including naming a few with powerful lobbying and interest groups on their side. For instance, Mr. Ramaswamy has done what few Republicans before him have: he has openly criticized the military's lack of accountability and compared it to the most egregious cases of fraud elsewhere in the Executive Branch.[142] In so doing, Mr. Ramaswamy and others pointed out an unpleasant truth: The defense industry is a major impediment to balanced budgets because it serves as a counterweight to calls for spending cuts. Likewise, President Trump criticized the disturbing trends and partisanship in the American military.[143]

If the recent conduct of the military brass is indicative of anything, it is that this bureaucracy thinks it is entitled to do whatever it wants without risking spending cuts and other punitive measures. Republicans are increasingly cognizant of the Pentagon problem, even if there were outliers like Nikki Haley and Chris Christie who want to uphold the business-as-usual approach. (Obviously, the House GOP's support for another budget-breaking DOD giveaway in the 2024 Defense Appropriations bill is a reminder that these problems exist outside of the Executive Branch.)[144]

Taken together, I think we ought to see the trends in the primaries as a huge vindication of the reformer instincts championed by President Trump when he was a candidate back in 2015 and

2016. Looking back, I think the trend is that the party leadership has come to embody the sentiments of the base. Put differently, I think that the mood of the Tea Party has become the identity of the GOP, which is a great development.

In sum, the Republican Party is changing, even if only rhetorical in the present. I am confident that in a few years, the priorities and policies embodied by President Trump, Mr. Ramaswamy, and Governor DeSantis—i.e., the goals and values that the voters prefer, including greater skepticism towards the defense industry and national security sphere, a refusal to go along to get along on ruinous bipartisan bills—will win out. But until that time, there is still work to be done.

Early Operations:
Removal, Retirement, and Relocation

With the resources and planning set out, the next item on the checklist for appointees in early 2025 will be to begin the process of draining the swamp. In practical terms, this means moving things and people out of D.C. in the most literal sense. Via Schedule F, many, many career bureaucrats who for so long enjoyed full and uncontestable job security will be redesignated and subject to removal. They will not be moved to another department with other responsibilities, nor will they be given free movement to another role. They will be terminated, and in many cases, their old jobs will be shuttered rather than filled with a replacement.

Schedule F is not enough on its own, however. Reformers should also strive to take seriously and implement a tactic President Reagan campaigned on but never implemented, namely the closing of federal agencies. Federal agencies are sinecures for progressives;

jobs typically pay an average of $124k.[145] This is a huge amount of money, and it is a direct wealth transfer to liberals who would likely struggle to find other work—and certainly at that rate in the realm of politics.

The retire versus repurpose distinction is key, and if we do not appreciate it, then whatever reforms we attempt during the next Republican administration can be easily reversed by the next progressive government. The place to start is on the case for retiring agencies and individuals.

Shrinking the government means reducing the workforce and limiting the mission of the federal government. For too long, Republicans have tried to repurpose progressive agencies to advance conservative ends. Putting in ostensible conservative policy experts at places like USAID and HUD makes some sense at a superficial level, but I think it has a bad track record in the real world.

Not only do conservative appointees often achieve nothing substantive during their tenure, but these progressive offices remain intact, meaning that they are fully prepared to return to their true purpose—pushing progressive policies—as soon as a Democratic appointee assumes a leadership role. The effect is that these progressive agencies and their progressive employees continue to get paid and can establish continuity across governments. This is sadly a great example of why nothing changes in D.C.

Even if it is only a speedbump, Republicans should try to close these offices and stall their work entirely while they control the Executive Branch. We are time-limited and politically constrained in what problems we can address with respect to the permanent bureaucracy. What makes more sense considering those realities: trying to commandeer a progressive system, or simply turning it off for four years (if not longer)? I think the latter is clearly preferable. In the following chapter we will discuss which agencies ought to be closed.

Sadly, we cannot simply shut down the entire modern Executive Branch. Conservatives must govern to institute positive reforms (as opposed to simply cutting off bad existing policies and offices), and that turns to the other side of the reform movement: personnel. In my view, this will be one of the most difficult tasks of the next Republican government, and I think it can only truly be addressed with better personnel, which will be a recurring theme (to the extent it is not already).

Appointees must be able to identify the relevant career staff that influences the policy-making and governing processes to isolate and (ideally) remove them. This is not nearly as easy as it sounds. I have spoken to numerous former appointees in the Trump Administration, as well as veteran reformers from prior Republican governments, and a sad and common story they tell me is that they worked with an informed career who "helped" them only to discover far too late into the term that they were retarding their efforts, not advancing them.

In my view, stealthy saboteurs only succeed because of an information gap. This type of principal-agent problem is deeply frustrating, but it is not insurmountable. Indeed, I believe that many of the developments on the political personnel side within the conservative movement will directly address this issue. Nonetheless, we must be vigilant to find out where these partisans are in the policy process. It can be difficult to determine, but with enough preparation and study, including learning from the best (or less-than-best) practices of prior appointees, we will better position ourselves for the task of finally exerting control over the Executive Branch.

The final point to mention is that, when we cannot solve problems by firing people or closing agencies, there is one last option available: moving departments and agencies outside of D.C. President Trump's decision to move the Bureau of Land Management (BLM) out west was a brilliant move, and one that ought to be replicated as often as possible by conservatives when they are in control of the Executive Branch. I know that I have discussed this a bit already, so I will not tread over worn ground. But I will add that this could be as disruptive as any termination, be it of an office or a person.

Institutions are shaped by the things in proximity to them, from people to markets. There is a reason that every department in D.C. is left-wing: the culture, the local government, and the people nearby are all progressive! Some departments cannot be closed, and not all the bad staff can be removed. But the department itself can be relocated. Putting truly essential agencies closer to their missions—say, putting the Environmental Protection Agency in Texas or Florida—would put career staff in far closer proximity to the stakeholders and interests that the agency is supposedly working for.

If Republicans can move people out of power in D.C. while moving political power out of D.C., then that will go a long way in limiting the power of progressives to commandeer the Executive Branch when it is supposed to be controlled by Republicans who win it via elections.

Thinking Bigger

Ideology and an outline are very important tools for reformers who want to finally change things in D.C. But there is a third component that will be discussed, some here and in detail within the next chapter, and that is a more substantive vision. Republican politicians are great at creating sound bites for their voters (and sometimes the media and their other opponents, too). What Republican politicians are *not* good at is expressing a clear vision of what they want to do when they hold political power.

I want to talk a bit here about what is necessary for a serious reformer's vision on challenging progressive power. So far, we have discussed some of the tools and methods for limiting progressive influence and authority within the Executive Branch, i.e., to allow for an equal opportunity to implement an agenda when a Republican is in the White House. Here, I want to sketch out some general ideas on what reformers can do to go on the metaphorical offensive. The place to start is in hiring, which is the opposite side of termination and equally important.

More stringent standards must be imposed in hiring within the Executive Branch, and hiring rules must not be subject to affirmative action and other discriminatory practices. Imposing hiring standards will translate into better services for the American people along with a more equitable distribution of opportunity. Today, hiring in the Executive Branch is informed by (if not driven by) affirmative action principles. The workforce is not representative of America at large—a point progressives love to make when it comes to certain Americans, but not others.

The racial composition of the federal workforce is one of those cases. Blacks are vastly overrepresented in the federal workforce: despite making up only thirteen percent of the population, blacks account for nearly twenty percent of the federal workforce.[146] Americans who identify as white are also overrepresented, although by a comparatively smaller three percent. And in contrast,

Asians, who achieve better than virtually every other group in competitive settings and markets within America, are represented about on par with their numbers in the larger population—a statistic that serves as a good indicator that something is wrong under the existing hiring regime. We want the best, brightest, and most accomplished in the bureaucracy. We need a system that makes it possible for those people to make their way to the top. The current arrangement does not do that.

Ending affirmative action policies in government will lead to a more balanced distribution of federal jobs. The likely result will be increases in Asian and Hispanic workers, and a decline in black workers, followed by a slight decline in people identifying as white. But ending affirmative action will not necessarily lead to hiring better employees. Another change ought to be the reimplementation of job-based testing to better promote the candidates best suited for particular, specialized jobs.

The overall principle that reformers should adhere to and advance in federal hiring is this: we want the best, most capable, and most objectively desirable candidates to work in the federal government. When hiring becomes more meritocratic, and when termination becomes a real possibility, the upshot is that there will be better inputs (more qualified employees) and better outputs (higher quality services). This is an easy argument to make, and Republicans should rush to advance these changes, particularly as they reduce the federal workforce. The joint result will be that there will be fewer but better employees.

Similarly, Republicans need to prohibit public sector unions from setting labor terms. During my time in the Trump Administration, I saw up close how strong these unions are; they can almost unilaterally set terms. But to use a more relevant example, consider that many federal workers have not returned to their offices since before the outbreak of COVID-19 in 2020.

Though this story has flown under the radar, many employees in Executive Branch departments have not returned to in-person work across the federal government. For example, a recent GAO report found that "17 agencies' headquarters buildings were at 25% capacity or less in the first 3 months of 2023."[147] One reason why so many federal workers have been able to stay at home is because unions have supported their preference to work from home; indeed, they have argued against calls to go back to the office, even as ever more ridiculous stories concerning abysmal customer service leak into the press. Responses for poor customer service often point to a lack of adequate funding as the cause for massive backlogs in customer facing government functions, such as the IRS being behind on at least 24 million tax returns with no real plan to address them.[148] Perpetual out-of-office work undermines productivity.[149] Before COVID-19, teleworking was a privilege. Today, it is treated as a right. One union leader told *Bloomberg News* that federal employees have successfully worked from home and would not be bullied into returning to work for political reasons.[150] Going into work is now a partisan issue in the federal government.

Breaking union power in the public sector would also promote consumer welfare (i.e., it would benefit the American people) while also limiting the influence of progressives in government. The added benefit is that reducing union power in the public sector will translate to less funding for Democrat candidates (unions always take care to financially support their allies), which in turn will likely improve the chances for Republican candidates in Congress.

These changes are relatively modest in that they simply seek to change the process for bringing in good talent and pushing out bad employees. Still, this is a clear vision, and I think it is a winning one. Republicans ought to champion these reforms, in part because it is likely to resonate with voters. But these are small points that ought to contribute to a larger vision of reform, restructuring, and revitalization. In the next chapter, I will defer to the ideas of the reformers that ran in the GOP Presidential Primaries. Reviewing some of the plans and ideas of the leading candidates from the 2024 primaries offers a nice way of appreciating where the conservative movement is heading, as well as the development of a larger vision for the GOP and the country.

CHAPTER 8

A LARGER FRAMEWORK

The Beginning of the Beginning

A party platform does not mean much, and it typically does not change in any significant way over the years. But the candidates in each cycle typically do change, and the ideas they run on can vary a great deal—sometimes departing sharply from the past. In certain cases, an effective, popular candidate may be able to shift the party platform, and in turn, the broader party's trajectory, and philosophy.

President Trump, Mr. Ramaswamy, and Governor DeSantis are three prominent candidates from the 2024 cycle whose ideas for a future conservative agenda broke with the *status quo* in numerous ways. It is my belief that these three individuals could all permanently redirect and remake important aspects of the conservative political philosophy in America generally and in the GOP.

In this chapter, we will talk in greater detail about how these candidates see America's problems and what they intend to do about them. Critically, these men and their ideas are a positive indicator of where the GOP is heading, which is towards radical reform as opposed to the norm of cheap talk while upholding the *status quo*.

Towards the end of the chapter, we will contrast the ideas of the reformers with those of other voices and candidates within the GOP. Doing so will be illustrative of the problem facing the party, i.e., that of a small minority trying to hold back the reformer tide in D.C.

Trump Term Two

Right now, it is certain that President Trump will be the Republican presidential nominee in 2024; and if the polling is any indication, he should beat Biden in the general election, too. President Trump easily won the primaries and, barring a health issue, will return to the White House. In other words, a second Trump Administration appears imminent. So, what would the sequel look like?

To get an idea of what the next Trump Administration will look like, let's look back on the first term. During President Trump's first term, he and his team accomplished a lot. If I had to pick a few great achievements that stand out among the many good achievements, I would highlight the following: President Trump secured relative peace in the Middle East (unthinkable today, given the ongoing war between Israel and Hamas) and Europe (Russia and Ukraine remain locked in conflict), along with low energy costs and a generally prosperous economy. And while he does not get credit for it, President Trump handled COVID-19 as well as possible via Operation Warp Speed, quickly pushing out a vaccine that was impactful for those in the at-risk categories.

To distill President Trump's first term into a sentence, life was good in Trump's America, and the world was a safer place.

Turning to specific policies, the former president's record is largely good. For instance, President Trump's tax cuts were a positive development, and his enforcement of immigration law was better for everyone, which contrasts sharply with Biden's disastrous open border approach. To be sure, there were letdowns, with the most obvious being the "criminal justice reform" bill, which was bad. (Consequently, there should be a concentrated effort to impose strict penalties on criminals during the next Trump Administration.)

Finally, the one big issue that President Trump struggled with, and which must be rectified in 2025, is checking the Deep State and the bureaucrats. This is not President Trump's fault, as he spent most of his first term fighting the lies of the Russia hoaxers, namely the journalists and their spook handlers who promoted it. He knows well how destructive the permanent government is, and he tried to address the issue in some ways during his presidency.

Unfortunately, the COVID-19 crisis precluded any serious effort to reform the civil service, among other governmental entities. But even then, President Trump did prepare for Schedule F, and moved BLM out of the Beltway. Finishing the job should be the focus in January 2025.

The good news is that President Trump has indicated that he is keenly interested in uprooting the bureaucratic class in a second term. Indeed, this is one of the policies that he clearly is deeply committed to and personally invested in. As it stands today, President Trump has discussed a handful of policies he will implement once in office.

So far, President Trump has promised to dismantle the national security architecture in Washington—a massive and badly needed step to check the influence of those in the Pentagon and throughout the Department of Defense.[151] In June of 2023, President Trump swore that he "will totally obliterate the Deep State." (He also joked that he would do what Biden did and investigate rivals who outperform him, a joke that reporters did not appreciate, and which they predictably melted down over.)

In terms of actual decisions and policies, reforming the Deep State will likely mean rescinding security clearances (which is long overdue, given the behavior of disgraced officials like James Clapper[152]), closing various jobs and offices, and firing career employees via redesignating their roles.[153]

The only way to end the abuses is to close up shop, so to speak, and to make sure that the offices themselves are shuttered, even if doing so merely hampers the next administration that tries to empower the same people and programs. (Sadly, this is a major issue with taking on the Deep State and the bureaucracy: most reforms can be easily reversed by a future administration. This problem gets greater attention in the following chapter, which outlines some of the risks and realities of trying to reform D.C.)

Given that large majorities of Republicans and Democrats in Congress are fully in support of the Pentagon and the numerous related national security offices in D.C. and around the country, it is unlikely that Congress would support cuts—let alone deep cuts—to these organizations (see the recent 2024 defense spending bill).

As such, President Trump may need to submit his own budget, or alternatively designate the relevant people as at-will before terminating them. In that case, there would still be money going into the agencies and departments, but there would be no way to spend it with the reduced number of employees. While this is probably not the most efficient way to trim the federal government, it may be the only workable path.

An additional step that the president should take is enforcing the Uniform Code of Military Justice (UCMJ), as doing so would provide a means of policing the bad behavior of partisan military officials who denigrated their offices when they slandered the president—which they may not legally do—in the form of denying them benefits and implementing punishments. There are several candidates whose bad actions are worthy of sanction under the UCMJ.[154] Enforcing the law against transgressors is morally right, and it might deter others from engaging in similar behavior in the future. And whether deservingly or not, this move will probably help the military to recover its diminished standing in the eyes of the American people.

Furthermore, President Trump has vowed to use the various administrative agencies as tools for shaping the actions of officials elsewhere in government, e.g., by using the Department of Justice to direct law enforcement officials to enforce laws against theft and assault that are currently being ignored by left-wing governments and officers in the states.[155]

Progressive critics have predictably called President Trump's tentative approach fascism, dictatorship, etc., which is of course false and hyperbolic. In fact, progressives do the very same thing when they are in power. The upshot is that conservatives have every right to use the Executive Branch as progressives do in 2025 and beyond. It is likely that reformers will be bolder and more committed to using executive power in the same regard.

I must also mention that President Trump has taken to heart some of the criticisms of his government during the first term. Specifically, he has acknowledged that personnel and coordination were real problems to the implementation of his campaign promises; he recently stated that these issues were primarily a consequence of his outsider status in politics: when he came to D.C., he didn't know anyone.[156] Thus, he had no choice but to rely on others, many of whom were interested in their own projects and ambitions.

The advancement of the MAGA agenda was turned over to RINOs, which in some respects represents a stolen election in its own right. This will not happen again.

Thankfully, President Trump understands the importance of personnel and is certain to approach the problem head-on in 2025. In other words, President Trump gets it. This is *his* last shot, and he will not allow others to mess it up for him again. And the good news is that he is not the only one who grasps this. President Trump has many more allies this time around.

The Outsider

Mr. Ramaswamy was one of the most interesting non-politicians to ever seek the GOP nomination. In fact, the only candidate in recent memory who was at all similar to Mr. Ramaswamy was then-candidate Donald Trump in 2015, which is high praise. Like President Trump, Mr. Ramaswamy has the unique capability to dominate a stage and communicate directly to his audience; he also has made great use of social media to complement his strong performances in more conventional media settings. He will no doubt continue to be a huge asset to President Trump and the reform effort as a surrogate for the Republican nominee; it is likely that he will serve in the next Trump administration in some capacity.

But Mr. Ramaswamy in 2023 is in some ways even more intriguing than then-candidate Donald Trump was in 2015: given his age (he is only thirty-eight years old) and striking achievements (he is worth close to $1b and has succeeded in one of the most difficult industries, biotech), he is one of the most accomplished candidates ever for his age. Moreover, Mr. Ramaswamy brought to the debates a sharp mind, a policy-driven focus, and an incredibly high level of verbal intelligence and humor that has resonated with Republican voters.

But beyond Mr. Ramaswamy's attractive attributes, his biggest contribution to the Republican primaries was on the policy side: he articulated an eclectic conservative agenda that in many ways merges the populist tone of President Trump with the libertarian sensibilities of a prolific private-sector entrepreneur.

To begin with, Mr. Ramaswamy fleshed out in systematic detail many of the critiques of the DEI racket and its attempt to commandeer markets and institutions to push left-wing politics. Specifically, his books *Woke, Inc.: The Social Justice Scam* (2021) and *Nation of Victims: Identity Politics, the Death of Merit, and the Path Back to Excellence* (2022) outline the now fully matured threat of DEI to markets, civil society, and meritocracy. These books are essential reading for anyone who wants to understand how the left wing took over the corporate boardroom.

Mr. Ramaswamy paid close attention to the pernicious impact the woke agenda has had on corporations, which today are more concerned with promoting Environmental, Social, and Corporate Governance (ESG)—i.e., investing other people's money in progressive social causes to subsidize their rent-seeking behavior—over profits to shareholders.

Making a profit for shareholders, Mr. Ramaswamy observed, is the entire point of investing. That we have moved so far from this simple premise is an indication of how widespread the rot is in the corporate boardroom—a point which helps to explain the insane response corporate America had to the George Floyd situation, the summer of BLM, and the 2020 Presidential Election.[157] Progressives have successfully captured this important institution.

One of Mr. Ramaswamy's key insights is that the transformation of the corporate boardroom was not natural, i.e., the end of an inevitable process. Instead, it was a man-made, orchestrated outcome of political design. Laws and norms helped to push this once non-political entity far into the realm of politics. The silver lining is that what has been molded by politics can be reformed by the political process. Truncating affirmative action and promoting non-discrimination principles will be instrumental in divesting progressives of corporate power.

Unsurprisingly, reasserting shareholder control is a big theme of Mr. Ramaswamy's work (a theme that mirrors his position on reasserting civilian control of the government), but so is the focus on the other aspects of progressive social engineering. Mr. Ramaswamy is a staunch critic of affirmative action,[158] the anti-policing/pro-crime measures instituted by Democrats in America's biggest cities, and the attempts by progressives to normalize and idealize LGBTQ lifestyle choices.[159] Promoting pro-social norms and policies are integral to Mr. Ramaswamy's policy vision for reforming America.

Throughout the campaign, Mr. Ramaswamy also took issue with the ineptitude of the federal government, promising to unilaterally shut down counterproductive agencies, like the Department of Education, USAID, and the Food & Drug Administration, while also abolishing collective bargaining for public sector employees.[160] He also wants to adjust the voting age while requiring civic literacy to vote, two proposals that progressives are predictably freaked out about.[161] Put simply, he understands that these agencies and rules are bad for the American people and serve only to provide income to progressives. Mr. Ramaswamy has promised to end the rent-seeking in D.C. that makes progressive politics viable.

Mr. Ramaswamy went even further, however, promising to effectively cut off all funding for progressive causes and organizations. To use another example, he promised to fully support American energy producers while cutting off funds for unrealistic and ineffective green "alternatives" that will never deliver a viable—let alone economical—alternative to oil and natural gas. Turning off the government subsidies to these projects will cause them to crash; they are only pursued in the first place because they have the financial backing of the state.

Indeed, Mr. Ramaswamy's campaign acknowledged a basic truth about progressive politics (that conservatives inexplicably do not discuss nearly enough), which is that these left-wing institutions, nonprofits, initiatives, and "public markets" exist only because they are given free money by the government, or have rules enforced by the state that benefit them and their respective enterprises. When the money gets shut off, these organizations and initiatives will fail and disappear. Destroying these left-wing entities must be part of any serious reformer's agenda.

To be clear, while the general tone of Mr. Ramaswamy towards the Deep State and the bureaucracy is not that different from President Trump's stance, he actually goes much further.

As noted above, shutting down agencies may only be possible by redesignating employees to at-will. Likewise, closing agencies would require enormous firings. Mr. Ramaswamy understands that and has been very open about what is required to truly reform the federal government. President Trump must be cognizant of this reality and firm in his conviction to see these changes through in his second term, no matter the political costs in the immediate, e.g., losing an election cycle. America will benefit from having Mr. Ramaswamy's leadership in a second Trump administration to implement these reforms.

Similarly, Mr. Ramaswamy took aim at one of D.C.'s most corrupt and protected institutions: the military. The Pentagon has recently become a hive of left-wing social engineering, but it has always been a hub of waste, fraud, and abuse. (Establishment Republicans in D.C. are happy with this situation, and do not want to disrupt DoD in any meaningful way.)

The Pentagon is a microcosm of D.C.: nothing changes there, no matter who is elected or what they run on. This is an obvious and uncomfortable truth for many. But not Mr. Ramaswamy; he relentlessly attacked the military bloat for months, basically by himself, as well as the myriad globalist policies it has promoted for decades. A big reason for this is that he is not dependent on the support of government contracting firms for financial support in elections.

Furthermore, by vigorously criticizing the Department of Defense's inflation of threats, which has led to more chaos abroad than security at home (though it has contributed to the general decline in civil liberties for American citizens), Mr. Ramaswamy lambasted the failed foreign policy of the Department of Defense along with its bad conduct.[162]

Like President Trump, Mr. Ramaswamy has argued for the adoption of an "America First" foreign policy strategy of promoting our interests first and foremost while eschewing the supposed "post-war order" (which has generally created disorder) and its many pricey obligations for American taxpayers.

As one might expect, Mr. Ramaswamy, like President Trump before him, has incurred serious blowback for stating these obvious facts about the problems with the Pentagon and with American foreign policy. Some in the GOP, like Nikki Haley[163] and Chris Christie, have disagreed with Mr. Ramaswamy for stating that Ukraine is not in America's national interest.[164] But Mr. Ramaswamy's point that NATO expansion has had the effect of seeking conflict with Russia and pushed it closer to China has proven true despite efforts by serious statesmen like the late Henry Kissinger, who spent his career trying to prevent such a problematic and fearful outcome.[165]

To give greater detail to what has already been stated, Mr. Ramaswamy has articulated a clear, realist vision for the US in world affairs: protect our interests to the best of our ability and mitigate where we can so that we can limit entanglements outside the American sphere. As such, he has pushed for increasing American financial and technology independence by developing better semiconductor manufacturing at home and deterring China in the immediate from attacking Taiwan.[166]

While some have criticized this strategy, in truth, America's interest in Taiwan is largely driven by technological and economic concerns, meaning that our interest in helping Taiwan to defend itself against potential Chinese aggression will decline once we have shored up our interests.

These are sensible policies that as one can imagine have incensed neoconservatives and more globalist Republicans who see America's supposed duty to police the world as nonnegotiable and the highest priority. America's duties are more limited, and if we want to give our problems with the budget and the debt the due consideration they deserve, then at some point we will need to address defense spending. Mr. Ramaswamy's vision, if

implemented, offers a means of finally addressing those twin economic issues.

In sum, Mr. Ramaswamy set out and ran on a distinct view
for the future conservative agenda. It is a good omen that he was
and remains popular with conservative voters, as it shows that
they have an appetite for real change and substantive policy—two
things that they get little from when it comes to the traditional
Republican candidate. Mr. Ramaswamy made a tremendous
impact on the GOP this cycle, and I am confident his influence
will grow as a senior official and administrator in the next Trump
Administration. Turning from Mr. Ramaswamy's view for the
country, we will look next at Governor DeSantis.

The Florida Model

There is a strong argument that Governor DeSantis has accomplished as much during his tenure as governor of Florida as perhaps
any governor in America over the last fifty years. Very intelligent
and well-read on the relevant facts, issues, and rules of government, Governor DeSantis had all the requisite tools to bring his
governing strategy from Florida to 1600 Pennsylvania Avenue.
While he did not perform as he might have liked in the primaries,
Governor DeSantis nonetheless ran a strong campaign and made
real contributions to the reform movement.

In some respects, Governor DeSantis is the opposite of Mr.
Ramaswamy and President Trump. Where the latter two entered
politics later in their lives, Governor DeSantis has been involved
in public affairs for his entire career. From serving in the military
as a lawyer for the Navy Judge Advocate General's Corp (JAG) to

working in Congress, Governor DeSantis has always been involved in public service and the promotion of conservative causes.

During Governor DeSantis's time in office, Florida has enacted an almost entirely positive conservative agenda, from cutting taxes to eliminating left-wing educational programs and priorities, to the funding of and support for local police. Governor DeSantis's government has focused on serving its constituents by providing quality governance and trimming unnecessary, fatty programs that suck up taxpayer dollars with no benefit to the public, e.g., just look at his record on taking on the critical race theory education racket.[167] Many governors could learn from his example.

Governor DeSantis stood out in the primaries as one of the few elected officials to meaningfully push back on the craziness of the Biden Administration. For instance, he expressed skepticism towards the CDC and Dr. Fauci at the height of the COVID-mania in 2020 and 2021 when most politicians simply deferred to the experts. Indeed, maybe the biggest point in Governor DeSantis's favor is that he has been willing to and capable of taking on entrenched left-wing bureaucracies, especially in the education sphere.[168] In short, he has used the power of his office to counter established progressive forces in Florida politics.

Likewise, Governor DeSantis has taken steps to counteract the most egregious actions of the Biden Administration. The obvious example is on immigration, where Biden and Co. have refused to follow federal immigration law. (As it stands today, over 4 million illegal immigrants have entered the country under Biden's tenure, bringing the total number of illegal immigrants in the country to well over 8 million.[169])

Governor DeSantis has done what Biden will not do, which is protect the American people from illegal immigration. Where the

Biden Administration has done everything to violate immigration law and to encourage unlawful entry, the DeSantis Administration has gone to equally great lengths to protect Floridians from the many costs associated with illegal immigration, e.g., by sending illegal immigrants to the communities that do not want immigration law enforced.

In a perfect world, Governor DeSantis could enforce immigration law from Florida, but existing Supreme Court decisions preclude that option. Instead, he has taken the next-best option, which is to put progressives in closer proximity to their desired policies. The results are clear: progressives themselves do not like illegal immigration when they incur the costs, and the recent polling reflects that reality.[170]

The case of illegal immigration is a microcosm of the DeSantis Administration's approach to dealing with progressive lawlessness: get creative to shift costs legally and efficiently to those creating problems, i.e., the Democrats. One way to think about the DeSantis government is that it has guarded Floridians from asymmetric risks generated by the illegal acts of Biden and Mayorkas at DHS by sending illegal immigrants to communities that supported Biden and are nominally in favor of illegal immigration—at least when Republican states are stuck with the costs.[171]

At the same time as Governor DeSantis has promoted good governance, cut off rent-seekers, and countered progressive lawlessness at the national level, he has turned Florida into a ruby red state.[172] And Governor DeSantis has done so with support from traditional Republicans to moderates, and even some Democrats. Florida boasts a strong economy, low crime, and a growing population, which evidences its appeal to Americans around the country (something that cannot be said for New York and California).[173]

Governor DeSantis's landslide reelection in 2022 was a referendum on the reformer movement, and voters were clear: they liked the change and wanted more of it.

If there is a single thread that connects the various decisions that Governor DeSantis has made in his time in office, it is this: he has consistently sought to trim the power of progressives within the Florida state government while simultaneously promoting basic good governance policies. This is not some obscure science, and it works.

As an aspiring presidential candidate for the Republican Party, Governor DeSantis promised voters that he would bring his Florida model to Washington, D.C. if he is elected. Central to that promise is the idea that the power of the governor's office will translate to the power of the president. In theory, this is surely correct. This is, after all, the original constitutional arrangement: the executive is a unitary office; everyone involved works for the president. But as we have discussed elsewhere, the original Constitution is no longer the law of the land; and the structure it created is not exactly in effect these days.

I bring this up not to push back on the vision of Governor DeSantis—far from it. I am a strong supporter of his plan for the country and his approach to executive power. Rather, I am a bit skeptical about the claims by the governor, as well as those of President Trump and Mr. Ramaswamy, that Republicans *can* or *will* be able to legally use presidential power. As we have seen, presidential power and influence is a one-way ratchet in Washington, D.C.: progressives may aggressively employ it to advance their political ends while Republicans have no such capacity to do so.

The final vision to discuss for the GOP and the country perhaps reflects that darker reality, i.e., that there really is not much room for reformers in D.C., so there should not be any real effort to change the *status quo* in a meaningful way.

Actually, Everything Is Fine

The final perspective to discuss comes primarily from Governors Haley and Christie, the two Establishment candidates who ran real campaigns in the 2024 primary cycle (no offense to the other candidates in the Establishment Lane). There are differences between these two when it comes to certain issues, but they broadly share a view of the country and agree as to what can (and cannot) be done, and thus what ought to be prioritized. Consequently, it is not worthwhile to highlight the ways in which they are distinguishable from each other.

These candidates were relatively open about the fact that they were not running on reforming anything, at least not in a meaningful way. Instead, they simply emphasized that they would "restore" various corrupt institutions, e.g., the DOJ and DOD, without any explanation for what that would look like, or how it would avoid a reversion to the crooked mean when the next Democrat wins the presidency.

Similarly, these two were quick to praise the "brave men and women" in the bureaucracy who do their jobs without imposing their partisan views on their work. Sure, this is admirable, but it is also a cheap cop-out to avoid discussing the fact that there are very bad actors whose behavior has contributed to the sorry, badly broken nature of D.C., which is prominent throughout the Executive Branch. Highlighting a few cases of good behavior does not offset the manifest and substantial bad behavior in these agencies.

One interpretation of this rhetoric is that Christie and Haley wanted to appeal to moderates and thus want to send out a positive message. This is possible, but I think that their status as Establishment Republicans/RINOs gives a better account, especially when one considers that they are running in a primary, meaning that they are trying to appeal to *Republican voters*.

That is, these people understand how D.C. works; they may believe that there is sadly little hope of bringing about any kind of serious constitutional restoration. As such, they wanted to be realistic and, in a sense, honest by campaigning not on challenging the system, but instead by operating effectively within it (whether they can do even that is doubtful). Put bluntly, they do not think D.C. can be managed or fixed.

This is a sad, dark point, and one that I will expound on in the next chapter. But the basic idea is that candidates like Haley and Christie have little hope left in the ability of a reformer to change much of anything meaningful in the country. Given the track record of Republican presidents in D.C.—Ronald Reagan included, who is still hailed as a radical who transformed D.C.—one can see why they take this pessimistic approach.

The upshot is that these candidates campaigned on a few small but attainable goals, such as increasing funding to the Pentagon and sanctioning foreign terrorist organizations. They did not campaign on reforming politics at home because they knew that they themselves are incapable of changing anything. At the same time, they doubt the capacity of others to bring about political and cultural change in D.C.

To call this perspective bleak would be an understatement. But it captures the outlook of many powerful Republicans, like Mitch McConnell and basically every other Republican congressional leader in my lifetime. And while I am not a fan of Haley or Christie, their view deserves consideration because it is genuine and, terrifyingly, perhaps correct.

In the final chapter, I will discuss the possibility that these grand visions for reforming Washington are illusory. In such a situation, there are nonetheless changes to pursue, albeit far more limited ones than we might hope for. I turn next to this more negative outlook.

CHAPTER 9

THE LONGER GAME

What If Reform Is off the Table?

In the previous chapter, we discussed the various visions and plans held up and advanced by the serious, reformer 2024 candidates for the Republican presidential nomination. We talked a lot about the hopeful, positive ideas set out by President Trump, Mr. Ramaswamy, and Governor DeSantis, including breaking up federal agencies, asserting federal control over the city of Washington, D.C., and taking steps to destroy the accumulated unconstitutional power in the Executive Branch. They all want the same thing, which is to restore the traditional constitutional order and, necessarily, to reduce the power of the federal government.

At the same time, we talked very briefly about the Establishment Republican program embodied in the campaigns of Governors Christie and Haley—people whose plans are, frankly, uninspiring for those who want to restore the Constitution and reduce the power of rogue agencies and bureaucrats. One need only listen to one of their speeches to understand that the program they are selling is politically limited; their campaigns are relics of the short-sighted world of 2012 GOP politics.

The critical distinction is that the Establishment wing of the Republican Party does not promise to resolve the enduring and constitutionally existential problems within the political and governmental systems of Washington, D.C. To use a familiar illustration, their campaigns seek to put a band-aid on a grievous injury; in other cases, they ignore the problems altogether.

This is true of Governors Haley and Christie, but it is by no means limited to them: the same attitude is held by most Republicans in the Senate and a majority in the House. Instead of presenting broad plans for challenging the *status quo*, these Republicans argue for marginal efficiency and nominally better governance, e.g., a better funded Pentagon and the like. In other words, the Republicans in this category claim that they will get better results out of a sub-optimal situation. But make no mistake: the underlying situation—namely a bloated, unaccountable, and dubiously legal Executive Branch—is here to stay if these people can win power.

I understand why this message of efficiency over change is appealing to some, but for those who believe that things are badly broken in D.C., this is an unacceptable position to take because it is fundamentally a compromise with an egregious political and legal situation.

If the last few years (if not the last few decades) have shown us anything, it is that the trajectory of federal power is existential for conservatives. Every year, the original Constitution grows more foreign and irrelevant as the state gains power and becomes more intrusive, with bureaucrats asserting greater claims to intervene in the decisions of communities, businesses, customers, and what remains of civic life.

And each year, the agents of the federal government become more willing than ever to abuse the power of their office to help progressives and to hurt conservatives. This happened under Nixon, Bush, Obama, Trump, and Biden. To date, bureaucrats in D.C. have broken the law (as well as various norms) to help progressives, and they have done so without any accountability or fear of sanction. The list is long, but for a refresher, simply review the previous chapters.

Nonetheless, the promise of Establishment Republicans to "make D.C. work" (to put it simply) is still a promise to do *something*. Moreover, based on my own experiences in Washington, I am forced to conclude that the Haleys and Christies of the world may truly believe that what they are promising is all that they can deliver.

For instance, I had many conversations with well-intentioned people on Capitol Hill who, when pressed as to why they were unwilling to go harder at an issue, would say that essentially there are hard limits to what is possible, e.g., pushing hard on an issue could hurt the likelihood of getting cooperation from Democrats on another issue. The upshot is that we should be content going with the small "win" over no win or even an internecine victory.

Put differently, Establishment Republicans believe that political realities are fixed, so we must try to make the best with what we have, as it were. Thus, any push for sizable reforms or even radical, constitutional transformation is futile. We cannot really reduce the size of the government, so we should not waste time discussing what cannot be done. This outlook puts a very rigid boundary around the political options available when negotiating with Democrats. Consequently, this means that we cannot really hope to reduce the power of the federal government.

Before delving further into this more pessimistic outlook, I want to clarify that I decided to save this topic for the end of the book because I think it represents the strongest argument against the reformer instinct and ideology that I have pushed for throughout.

There are, of course, bad-faith Establishment Republicans who have ulterior motives for opposing reform, e.g., elected officials who do not want to shrink the budget for the DoD because government contractors subsidize their campaigns or promise them seats on their boards in retirement (often they are also lucrative investors in defense companies). But I do not think this represents the majority of such people. Instead, I think there are many Republicans in D.C. who feel that the architecture of government is in part their legacy or the legacy of their party, and they consequently do not want to touch it (think about proponents of NATO and "America's role in the world").

And there are also those who may wish they *could* restructure the state, but believe that such a move is impossible given the development of the Executive Branch, the necessities, and obligations of the government, etc. Typically, such people present themselves as firm constitutionalists, albeit with a huge cutout for most of the dubious constitutional transformations of the twentieth century—that all gets a pass.

Appreciating this difference is instructive for grasping the extent to which the reformer, America First Republicans—DeSantis, Trump, Ramaswamy—break with the globalist-oriented Establishment Republicans: the former wants to change things and are willing to break with the past while the latter is loyal to the institutions and commitments made before, and have made peace with the system as it exists because they believe that certain things must be done (e.g., defense spending must go up), which precludes more radical change in the form of, say, acutely slashing federal spending everywhere.

As one might imagine, this is a sharp divide. And much as I identify with the reformers in the America First wing, there is a serious argument on the other side. It is only fair that I give it its due for you, the reader, to consider.

Political Realities

The pro-*status quo*, Establishment Republican program is, in my view, built around a few truths. While I disagree with the outcomes that these people come to re: politics, I do not dispute the (at least partial) validity of these principles.

First, the political system as it exists today runs on (or is retarded by) inertia. What has happened in the past basically constrains the political choices available to us in the present. This is true of the budget, and it is true of foreign policy. The nature of our political system, with its susceptibility to lobbying and partisanship, is such that the dead hand of the past guides our politics in the present and in the future. Real change is thus hard to come by indeed.

Second, the current constitutional system is (or appears to most Americans to be) legitimate. As such, there is no serious path available to restructure it, let alone to restore an older Constitution that many Americans—perhaps even most Americans—have no ties to. The changes instituted by the New Deal and Civil Rights revolutions cannot be undone, and the trajectory of political power from the states and Congress to the Executive Branch (and to a lesser extent the Judicial Branch) will not be reversed. Any dream of civic renewal and a return to local government is just that, a dream.

I think there is a lot of truth in this point. One way to conceptualize this point is through a thought experiment: Given the liberal to moderate views of the Bush family, is it more or less likely that H. W. Bush and George W. Bush would have nominated Justices Thomas and Alito, respectively, to the Supreme Court had they fully known their jurisprudential outlooks? Based on their public views on everything from social justice to policy, my instinct is to say no. In other words, we got very, very lucky that these squishy Republicans nominated excellent judges who are willing to vote for decisions that seek to restore the original Constitution.

Third and probably most importantly, the extant political system is self-interested and jealous, and the actors within it are either rapacious (the president and courts) or pusillanimous (Congress). Any attempt to disrupt its continuity will be quashed—including by conservatives in positions of power. Probably the strongest example of this is the infamous decision in *National Federation of Independent Business (NFIB) v. Sebelius.* In that case, the conservative Chief Justice John Roberts wrote a majority opinion upholding the Affordable Care Act (ACA) and did so by twisting the law to avoid a truly originalist outcome.

So, why did Roberts uphold the ACA? The simple explanation is that, had he not done so, then the logic of an opinion invalidating the law on originalist grounds would potentially open up the existing constitutional order to a slew of attacks. While it might be cynical, there is a logic to Roberts' decision, and it is a microcosm of an attitude that is prevalent throughout the Republican Establishment, i.e., that there are limits to the reforms conservatives wish to pursue. Moreover, his decision is consistent with his other votes, i.e., he has voted elsewhere to avoid politically explosive and originalist outcomes, even when doing so has put him at odds with his prior voting record.

For further evidence, look back on the 2020 Election shenanigans. None of President Trump's cases were taken up on the merits; instead, courts—including conservative courts filled with Trump appointees—did everything possible to dismiss cases on procedural grounds. Never mind that there was open evidence of actions by progressives to violate state constitutions to illegally change election laws, sometimes *during the elections themselves*. Conservative judges—indeed, the supposedly "best and brightest" within the Federalist Society—went to impressive lengths to avoid the actual legal issue(s) and to lambaste President Trump[174] for exercising his right to petition the courts for redress.[175]

The main takeaway is that many conservatives (certainly a majority in D.C.) do not want to upset the proverbial apple cart that is the existing political system, let alone the myriad legal rules and developments that underpin it. It is certain that, if a Republican pushed maximally hard on reforming the federal government, these people in the Establishment Republican orbit would acquiesce to progressive attempts to enjoin, limit, or reverse any meaningful, radical reforms; I doubt they would offer any real pushback. The sad saga of successful, one-way lawfare in D.C., going back to at least the Watergate scandal, is a testament to this truth.

Now, whether progressive and Republican resistance would translate to elected GOP officials coming out of the woodwork, to condemn attempts at reform, or nominally originalist judges finding arcane justifications for protecting progressive rent-seekers and policies, is irrelevant. Rather, the point is that the dominant forces in American politics would ensure that nothing changes in D.C. or in the country. The post-war order must live on, and so too must the myth of a constitutional republic.

None of this is uplifting, and while I think that some of these assumptions might be a bit misguided, the D.C Republicans do appear to be basically correct in their assessment about D.C.'s resistance to change and in turn the limits on reform.

For me personally, I took a more negative view when I saw the absurdity of the Comey witch-hunt up close; it was obviously spurious and partisan, and yet Republican senators fell in line to defend the FBI and DOJ, many going on television to engage in moral grandstanding about importance of impartiality and the rule of law.

Looking back, I see these outbursts as sad examples of a certain kind of learned behavior by D.C. Republicans; it is an unthinking reaction to defend obviously egregious abuses in the name of "national security" and supposed stability. Far too many elected Republicans jump at the opportunity to behave in this way, especially if they get the opportunity to do so on *Face the Nation* or another progressive television show.

So long as prominent figures in the media say that a future Republican president, be it Donald Trump, Ron DeSantis, or someone else, is engaged in racism or corruption as opposed to actual reform, a sizable chunk of the party's elected officials in D.C. will respond not with counterarguments but with attacks against the White House. There is the reason that D.C. Republicans fall for basically every major hoax and moral panic, be it COVID-19, the George Floyd/Black Lives Matter saga, the IntelGate/Russia lie: they are risk averse, not especially smart, and eager to follow the media.

The point of all this ranting is to say that the Christies and Haleys in the party who seek leadership roles do understand Republican Party politics well. Thus, their respective decisions to campaign on the few things they can change, e.g., sending more money to the Pentagon or building additional military bases abroad, is honest and defensible, even if the policies themselves do not advance the well-being of American citizens.

I often wonder what will happen when a reformer gets to D.C. and pushes as hard as he or she can to reform the system by bringing it back in sync with the Constitution. President Trump attempted this on a few things and was handicapped and betrayed by his own party in so many ways that he never had an opportunity to exert the necessary pressure to enact deep and lasting reforms. And there are reasons to wonder if such an approach is even possible.

So, what if the Establishment Republicans are right?

Dare to Try: The Big Issues

The Establishment Republicans might be right about what is politically possible. But we can test their theory, and we should. The plan is simple. The next Republican administration must push maximally hard on promoting and implementing policies to drain the swamp. Setting up a real confrontation with the Deep State and its bureaucratic allies will clarify what is possible by way of reform politics.

Republicans must take these steps. The reality is that the *status quo* spells doom for the Republicans: we are currently unable to use the full constitutional power of the Executive Branch while progressive institutions and insiders steer the proverbial ship whether Democrats hold the presidency or not. Each year, progressives become further entrenched.

At the same time, Republicans cannot punish malfeasance and bad actors among the bureaucratic class who interfere in presidential transitions, undermine the rule-making process, and sabotage the implementation of the agenda a president ran and won on. The sad outcome is that our election system means very little. To use a sports metaphor, when we win elections, our team doesn't show up; when Democrats lose elections, their team never leaves.

Indeed, the upshot is that when we win elections, we do not get the full benefits of holding office. This sad situation seriously undermines the purpose of elections as well as the original constitutional system (to the extent it still exists today as a fragment of what it once was). Reformers must be focused on this overarching issue of constitutional restoration because it is the real threat to American democracy.

And the other side of the issue is equally bleak: Democrats can win elections and no matter how incompetent the president, and no matter how ridiculous their Executive Order, he or she will be protected and supported by the entrenched powers in D.C., which will work to implement the rule, guidance, etc. Again, just look at the Biden Administration.

Joe is obviously infirm if not senile, and the Executive Branch moves with precision and effort to enact every single one of his left-wing programs, all while protecting Biden and covering for his mistakes. Contrast this situation with that of President Trump: he was sabotaged nonstop, and his moderate Executive Orders (some simply rescinding those of President Obama) were fought by bureaucrats in protracted and illegal battles.[176]

What should be clear by now is that whatever the merits of the Establishment Republican view, it is untenable and insufficient. We must enact radical change to reform the federal government. Even if all we can do is try, try we must.

As we have discussed throughout the book, personnel decisions are critical, and so is planning, and we need both to reestablish control over the Executive Branch. Moreover, we need candidates with big visions and even greater resolve to see their reforms through. Stewardship, fortitude, and competence are essential.

As I see it, there are a few big picture agenda items. First, we must end D.C. home rule. All the major reform candidates have discussed this idea. Separate even from illegally sanctioning (and now rewarding) the rioting during the 2020 Black Lives Matter-Floyd saga, politicians in D.C. have failed their constituents and the basic requirements of governance.[177] This is an anti-social choice that D.C. voters are too stupid and ideological to fix. We need to arrest criminals and put them away for a long time. It is that simple.

Failing to police crime has real consequences. For instance, crime has spiked like never before in D.C., so much so that its professional sports teams are leaving the city.[178] Policing is nonexistent, and crime is pervasive to the point that it is hurting the ability of popular sports teams to make money.

Consequently, the move out of the city is a no-brainer, and it is also an indictment of the dysfunction in D.C. Given the somehow positive legacies of "public servants" like Marion Barry (who remains popular with liberals to this day), I see no reason to believe that any of this will ever change.[179]

Thankfully, D.C. was always meant to be an administrative region to house the federal government. The next Republican president must return D.C. to its original purpose, which will be to the benefit of all parties. This misguided experiment in democracy/ self-rule was a mistake, and it should be corrected.

Similarly, returning Arlington and Alexandria to D.C. should be on the table; this would better capture the reality that these towns (full of government workers and contractors) are part of the larger city while also helping Virginia electorally by excising two of the most progressive parts of the state.

The second step to break up progressive power is to move agencies out of D.C., e.g., the Bureau of Land Management (BLM) and the FBI. For reasons discussed earlier, such a move would be better for the agencies and their missions while simultaneously cutting back on the number of jobs in D.C. for progressives. Such a move will inject new blood, so to speak, into these agencies.

On the issue of personnel, the next Republican president must quickly reclassify and retire (or fire) bureaucrats with influence on policy. This will allow the Executive Branch to shed ideological deadweight, which in turn will allow the president to better implement the agenda voters supported which put him into office.

Similarly, it is imperative that the next president replace the highest-ranking bureaucrats. Getting rid of the Anthony Faucis of the world will be key to ensuring that power within the Executive Branch does not swing to the unelected. Stated differently, the president should be the one calling the shots, not a career bureaucrat. Anything less than this is chaos.

The same is true of the military. The days of deferring to the supposed expertise of the Pentagon must end. The foreign policy disasters of the last few decades, and especially those of the Biden Administration, are proof that we cannot go on the same path with the same people.[180] Selecting a non-D.C. insider to run DoD is key, especially after the collapse in support for the American military as an institution. Understanding that the entire Beltway military class is self-interested and unreliable is necessary to institute meaningful reforms in this space.

Recent events again underscore this reality: Secretary Austin's unannounced disappearance due to an elective surgery, and the

Pentagon's refusal to disclose information on his status—to the president, Congress, or the people—is another outrageous scandal, and further proof of the autonomous, independent nature of the Executive Branch.[181] And as of the writing of this chapter, weeks later, we are still in the dark on what happened and why. This is bizarre and will change. We need new leaders who serve the president and the people, not their pocketbooks and egos.

The third and final overarching aspect of the reform agenda is to cut off progressive subsidies and rent-seeking. Weeding out DEI contractors and contracts is the low-hanging fruit. Every DEI workshop is a check for grifters who profit off woke drivel. These lecturers and experts are parasites sucking money from taxpayers to browbeat people on race, sex, etc. This can end very easily.

Rent-seeking exists in the world of NGOs, too. "Sue and settle" is an underhanded tactic used by public-interest groups that supposedly want to promote policies for the public benefit. These organizations use lawfare to extract public money from agencies to their pockets while also pushing their own personal policy goals.

Take HUD for example. HUD is powerful to the extent it provides conditional grants to localities to promote certain policies. But in practice, those grants aren't *really* conditional: NGOs find favorable judges and venues to take their side, meaning that they can get the grant money, defeat the policies of the political leadership, and often get the opposite programs funded. This arrangement is a genuine threat to democracy, and it is another piece of evidence in support of the thesis that in D.C., the progressives have rigged the game so that, no matter what, they will always win.

And this issue of self-interested NGOs extends beyond America's borders. Specifically, NGOs take advantage of institutions like USAID: they extract money from these institutions via grants to promote progressive ideological projects, and often the policy goals *they* push on foreign countries are sharply ideological and contentious in the US, too.[182]

The outcome is that America's standing around the world falls as it becomes associated with the craziest, most progressive social policies.[183] (Acting as an international harridan is not a winning strategy.) All the while, the NGOs sustain themselves; typically, they become even more aggressive and divisive with the progressive social policies they push.

But the rent-seeking is bigger than a lecture on why racism explains disparities between groups, or why certain jobs ought to be redistributed to unqualified candidates. Indeed, the biggest scams are the departments themselves. Entities like HUD and the Department of Education serve no conservative ends, and Republicans must be honest about that. Instead, they serve as landing pads for graduates of questionable undergrad institutions and the holders of insipid master's degrees, most of them affluent white liberal women with chips on their shoulders. These and other departments should be closed down when possible and handicapped otherwise.

For years, conservatives have talked about using these departments to push conservative policies and values. It never works. Shutting down these progressive slush funds will do far more good for taxpayers than any well-intentioned faith initiative or effort to promote the great books curriculum. To make a real difference, we must be realistic and honest about the current situation, which necessarily means internalizing that we cannot redirect these institutions to serve conservative ends. The best we can do is to simply close them down or retard their future use.

The Reckoning

To sum everything up into a single point, I think it would be useful to quickly reflect on my favorite movie, *Tombstone* (1993). For those who don't know, *Tombstone* is a Western loosely based on real events.

Set in the 1880s, the film centers around the timeless conflict between outlaws and the law. The plot is set in motion by an irreversible and egregious transgression against the law by the Cowboys (the outlaws' criminal gang). The act—the brutal and indiscriminate massacre of innocent people—is one of extreme defiance; it is intolerable, and it drives the bloody story forward.

In a famous scene, Doc Holliday (played by Val Kilmer) comments on the impending confrontation between the criminals and the lawmen who hunt them. Reflecting on the desire of Wyatt Earp to do justice to those who wronged him and his family, Holliday says: "Make no mistake, it's not revenge he's after. It's a reckoning."

The distinction between revenge and reckoning is important: where the former is more limited, i.e., rectifying a specific and personal wrong, the latter is different. Specifically, a reckoning is more capacious as it is not a particular or targeted desire to do justice. Instead, a reckoning, while also concerned with justice, is bigger: it is the correction of all former wrongs against a responsible party, not necessarily a single individual.

The subtext of *Tombstone* is that the prevalence of crime and the necessity of actors who often operated outside the law, were barriers to the development of a normal society in the West. The antisocial nature of crime, and the unusual methods necessary to bring justice to responsible criminals, were outliers in an otherwise modernized/modernizing country. Ending the madness and the patterns of illegality and excess was necessary to ensure social harmony, which in turn would go on to create prosperity.

Tombstone's distinction between revenge and reckoning is eminently applicable to the problem of D.C. and the Deep State in our time. It is not that one or even a few people misbehaved and deserve justice (though they do) for their illegal acts against President Trump, the Republican Party, and the American people.

Rather, it is that the entire political world and system in which these partisans operate is rotten and illegitimate. To fix D.C. and to meaningfully restore the constitutional order, the goal cannot be to bring a few lowly political hacks to justice. No, the end must be a reckoning—a constitutional reckoning.

For too long, our republican form of government has been mutilated and abused, so much so that its true form and purpose are unknown to most Americans (and to be sure, it is not taught in schools). This is why there must be a reckoning against the rival constitutional system constructed by FDR and added onto in the decades since. And this includes the aspects of the new political system that Republicans contributed to. It all must go.

Another key point that I must mention is that while an individual may be able to get revenge in a dramatic act of violence, a reckoning requires coordination and cooperation on a massive scale, thus the emphasis on planning, personnel, and teamwork. What is left of the Constitution is in mortal danger. To save and restore our political system, we must work together like never before to achieve certain crucial goals. This effort cannot be slapdash or impromptu.

And finally, if we are to turn the proverbial tide, then we must be willing to change our perspective on politics. In 2016, Mitch McConnell wrote a memoir called *The Long Game*. The book reflects on his career as the Republican leader in the Senate, and how he tried to understand politics in relation to his goals.

Whether one likes McConnell is irrelevant to his main point in the book, which is that to be effective in politics, one must look at the political landscape and one's goals from a more long-term view. This is clearly true.

But where I disagree with Senator McConnell is on how far one can look ahead. For McConnell, one must look at political goals in terms of elections and where they can eventually lead electorally and in turn, politically. But McConnell's understanding of politics is limited to the appointment and confirmation of judges who interpret the Constitution. Judges are of course powerful, but there are two other capable branches of government reformers can and must rely on to change D.C.

The upshot is that we should be looking further yet into the future. If Republicans can accomplish substantial reforms in the immediate period at electoral costs in the near future, but with better political prospects further down the line, then they should make that trade. This is especially true if Republicans can break the institutional power of progressives, which strengthens their election chances, among other things.

Democrats have long held this more distant view. Think about Obamacare: the ACA was extremely unpopular, and Democrats paid dearly for supporting it. But once the program was in place, no one would dare touch it. Nowadays, repealing the ACA is unthinkable. Democrats paid a lot in the immediate to fully entrench a program in the future.

Republicans must take the same view. Winning elections is a pointless exercise if the power gained from winning is never used effectively. For there to be a real reckoning, there must be an understanding that there is much to do, including many things which will harm Republicans at the polls in the present/future. Republicans must make peace with electoral blowback. No political change to the *status quo* is smooth and painless.

If Republicans can break the chain of subsidized benefits and jobs that progressives rely on to empower their base, then that will pay political dividends in the future. Similarly, if Republicans get nuked by the media for being "racist" and ending disparate impact rules that empower the progressive base, then they should do it nonetheless for the long-term windfall of weakening the left.

To undo the Administrative State, to defeat the Deep State, to end the grifting and corruption, Republicans must be willing to push as hard as they can to address a few narrow problems that, once resolved, will open new possibilities. For instance, we cannot hope to cut off progressive grifting and rent-seeking without first addressing the laws they wrote and enforce to this day against neutral, classical liberal principles. The list is extensive and goes on.

There is substantial work to be done, and not every problem can be solved with a couple magic words, like "you're fired." But that is not a bad place to start, and 2024 is as good a time as any to begin the arduous, year-long task of restoring our constitutional inheritance—the real one that our Founding Fathers left us, not the schizophrenic progressive constitution pushed on us.

I'm confident that if we can keep a few important ideas in mind—mission, personnel, perspective, and principles—then there is so much we can accomplish now that will position us for bigger future successes later.

Revenge is fleeting, but a reckoning is lasting.

ACKNOWLEDGMENTS

First and most importantly, I am grateful to my husband, Surya. I would not be who I am nor have done the things that I've done without you. I know that with you by my side and God in my heart, I can achieve anything. GMC. You remind me of this every day, and I love you with all my heart.

I would not have my love of country nor eye towards service without the example set by my parents. My father showed me the meaning of service before self and my mother demonstrated the power of "fearless love." My genius brother, Kyle, whose big brother antics made me tough, strategic, and helped me not take myself too seriously.

There is a saying in politics that if you want a friend in Washington, get a dog. But I would respectfully disagree. You may have to dig through a few rounds of people, but there are some good souls and devoted patriots that work in D.C., and I had the benefit of cultivating true friendships. Their words, ideas, impact, statesmanship, and patriotism are reflected throughout this book.

I am always grateful for the people who gave me those early shots on Capitol Hill, especially Kai and RJ. Also, my colleagues and trench-mates, especially Team Inhofe/EPW/and fellow "Airhead," that were with me in the fights on the Senate Floor, in the anterooms, and late night vote-aramas. The comradery established reflected our fearless team leader, Senator Jim Inhofe, who highlighted the importance of genuine friendship and trust, even with those with whom you vehemently disagree.

To my Team EPA colleagues, especially the early crew: Administrator Pruitt, Sam, Brittany, Sarah, and Justin. Expanding this out to our go-to White House crew, Mike, Francis, and Aaron. Your steadfast commitment to implementing the President's vision and burning the midnight oil, both here and abroad, minimized the many "bombs" thrown our way and demonstrated true perseverance.

Thank you to Alex for bringing the Capitol Hill gumption when I, and our team, needed it most. You have a knack for stepping in and stepping up to save the day. You are my 3 AM friend (Surya's too).

Thank you to David and Bill. Your entrance into EPA changed my life for the better in so many ways. From long-distance running advice to permitting reform, your quiet brilliance and expansive knowledge of all things "air" injected much-needed focus and produced targeted effectiveness. Every day working with you was a blessing, even the hard days.

Thank you to Administrator Wheeler for giving me the offer of a lifetime. Your patience, strategy, and kindness are what carried us all through a most difficult year (2020) . . . while also keeping our environmental progress on track! I'd say you more than deserve a second shot.

Shout out to the amazing comms experts I've worked with over the years, especially the two that walked me through my first live hit: Michael and James.

Just about all Trump appointees went through some version of Hell because we "deigned" to work for a man who bucked the elites and prioritized the needs of the American people. The courage required to sign up for this task and withstand the affiliated scrutiny is infectious. I hope and pray we may all get the chance to do it again.

Coleman, my researcher, number one creative, and editor for the book, your insights and skills with words are unmatched. I can't wait for you to use your skills as an official member of the Bar.

Sarah, the footnote expert and young conservative warrior who truly got this across the finish line, thank you.

I am grateful to my Bible Girls and Oxford community that have demonstrated the healing power of love, forgiveness, and SEC football—the perfect antidote to any scars from the Deep State.

And finally, to future generations of freedom fighters, including my darling loves, Scout and Rhyder. May this book be a guide and an inspiration to reinstate our original Constitution that left us all with a promise worth fighting for: "a more perfect union."

ENDNOTES

Chapter 1

1   Ellen Mitchell, "Defense Department Fails Another Audit, but Makes Progress," *The Hill*, December 2, 2022, https://thehill.com/policy/defense/3740921-defense-department-fails-another-audit-but-makes-progress/.

2   Lara Seligman & Connor O'Brien, "Conservatives Lash Out at the Military Over 'Woke' Policies," *Politico*, May 21, 2021, https://www.politico.com/news/2021/05/21/conservative-critics-military-policies-490197.

3   Linda Qui, "The Many Ways Trump Has Said Mexico Will Pay for the Wall," *New York Times*, January 11, 2019, https://www.nytimes.com/2019/01/11/us/politics/trump-mexico-pay-wall.html.

4   Mail Online Videos, "Is Trump Losing His Grip on Rural Voters? Poll Says Support is Slipping in Flyover Country Where One Out of Seven American Live," *Daily Mail*, October 9, 2017, https://www.dailymail.co.uk/video/news/video-1289008/Trump-dons-coal-miner-s-helmet-West-Virginia-rally.html?page=.

5   David Roberts, "Hillary Clinton's 'Coal Gaffe' Is a Microcosm of Her Twisted Treatment by the Media," *Vox*, September 15, 2017, https://www.vox.com/energy-and-environment/2017/9/15/16306158/hillary-clinton-hall-of-mirrors.

6   Richard A. Epstein, "Biden's Unlawful Re-Entry into Climate Accord," *Hoover Institution*, February 1, 2021, https://www.hoover.org/research/bidens-unlawful-re-entry-climate-accord.

7   Datoc, Christian, "White House Sparks Backlash after Saying High Gas Prices Guard 'Liberal World Order,'" *Washington Examiner*, July 1, 2022, https://www.washingtonexaminer.com/news/white-house/brian-deese-gas-liberal-world-order?utm_source=msn&utm_medium=referral&utm_campaign=msn_feed.

8   Liz Peek, "China's Rising Emissions Prove Trump Right on Paris Agreement," *The Hill*, June 5, 2018, https://thehill.com/opinion/energy-environment/390741-chinas-rising-emissions-prove-trump-right-on-paris-agreement/.

9   Jon K. Lauck, "Trump and The Midwest: The 2016 Presidential Election and The Avenues of Midwestern Historiography," *Studies in*

Midwestern History: Vol 3, No. 1, 2017, https://scholarworks.gvsu.edu/
midwesternhistory/vol3/iss1/1/.

10   Joe Stephens and Carol D. Leonnig, "Solyndra Scandal: Full Coverage of
Failed Solar Startup," *The Washington Post,* December 25, 2011, https://
www.washingtonpost.com/politics/specialreports/solyndra-scandal/.

11   Dan Merica, "Trump Gets 2 Scoops of Ice Cream, Everyone Else Gets 1—
and Other Top Lines from his *Time* Interview," *CNN,* May 11, 2017, https://
www.cnn.com/2017/05/11/politics/trump-time-magazine-ice-cream.

12   "Report: China Emissions Exceed All Developed Nations Combined,"
BBC, May 6, 2021, https://www.bbc.com/news/world-asia-57018837.

13   Let's not forget that Biden effectively ended #MeToo (or at least suspended
it for a time) after his decades of documented sexual harassment and assault
became inconvenient to his political ambitions.

Chapter 2

14   Richard A. Epstein, *The Classical Liberal Constitution: The Uncertain
Quest for Limited Government,* (Harvard University Press, 2017), https://
www.hup.harvard.edu/catalog.php?isbn=9780674975460.

15   David Bernhardt, *You Report to Me: Accountability for the Failing
Administrative State* (New York: Encounter Books, 2023).

16   Commerce, Justice, Science, and Related Agencies, "Rogers Remarks at
FY24 Budget Hearing for the Federal Bureau of Investigation (as Prepared)
– 118th Congress (2023-2025)," House Committee on Appropriations
– Republicans Congress), April 8, 2024, https://appropriations.house.
gov/news/statements/rogers-remarks-fy24-budget-hearing-federal-bureau
-investigation-prepared.

17   Jennifer Knox, "Defense Spending Reaches Record High as Pentagon Fails
Its Audit – for Fifth Time," *The Equation,* December 14, 2022, https://
blog.ucsusa.org/jknox/defense-spending-reaches-record-high-as-pentagon
-fails-its-audit-for-fifth-time/#:~:text=Since%20the%201990%20
Congressional%20mandate,%2C%E2%80%9D%20according%20to%20
Michael%20J.

18   David Moore, "Lawmakers Benefit From Booming Defense
Stocks," *Sludge,* https://readsludge.com/2021/08/23/
lawmakers-benefit-from-booming-defense-stocks/.

19   Cornell Law School, "Separation of Powers," Legal Information
Institute, accessed June 28, 2024, https://www.law.cornell.edu/wex/
separation_of_powers_0.

20 United States Court of Appeals for the District of Columbia Circuit, "West Virginia v. Environmental Protection Agency," *Oyez*, accessed June 28, 2024, https://www.oyez.org/cases/2021/20-1530.

21 James Madison, "Federalist 51," *National Constitution Center,* accessed June 28, 2024, https://constitutioncenter.org/the-constitution/ historic-document-library/detail/james-madison-federalist-no-51-1788.

22 David Sokol and Adam Brandon, *America in Perspective: Defending the American Dream for the Next Generation,* (New York: Post Hill Press, 2022).

23 Mari Jo Buhle, Paul Buhle, and Dan Georgakas, ed., *Encyclopedia of the American Left,* (New York: Garland Pub, 1990).

24 W. Elliot Brownlee, *Federal Taxation in America,* 3rd edition, (Cambridge, MA: Cambridge University Press, 2016).

25 "The First Income Tax," *The American Battlefield Trust,* accessed June 28, 2024, https://www.battlefields.org/learn/articles/first-income-tax.

26 Fuller Court, "Pollock v. Farmers' Loan and Trust Company," *Oyez*, accessed June 28, 2024, https://www.oyez.org/cases/1850-1900/157us429.

27 U.S. Constitution, art. 1, sec. 8.

28 "About the Senate; Senate Created," *United States Senate*, accessed June 30, 2024, https://www.senate.gov/artandhistory/history/minute/Senate_ Created.htm.

29 Michael Parrish, "Court Packing and Constitutional Revolution," *Bill of Rights Institute*, accessed June 30, 2024, https://billofrightsinstitute.org/ essays/court-packing-and-constitutional-revolution.

30 Richard Hanania, "The Law that Banned Everything," Hanania Newsletter, April 11, 2022, https://richardhanania.substack.com/p/ the-law-that-banned-everything.

31 Charles Stimson and Stephanie Neville, "Warrants to Spy on Trump Campaign Lacked Probable Cause, DOJ Admits," *The Heritage Foundation*, January 30, 2020, https://www.heritage.org/crime-and-justice/commentary/ warrants-spy-trump-campaign-lacked-probable-cause-doj-admits.

32 Shannon Mullen, "New Information Raises Questions About FBI Raid on Catholic Father of 7," *Catholic News Agency*, September 25, 2022, https://www.catholicnewsagency.com/news/252385/ mark-houck-fbi-arrest-abortion-clinic.

33 Alyce McFadden, "Unions Spent Big to Boost Biden. Will He Return the Favor?" *Open Secrets*, February 19, 2021, https://www.opensecrets.org/ news/2021/02/unions-spent-big-boost-biden/.

34   Richard Hanania, "The Law that Banned Everything," *Hanania Newsletter,* April 11, 2022, https://richardhanania.substack.com/p/the-law-that-banned-everything.

35   Terry Martin, *The Affirmative Action Empire: Nations and Nationalism in the Soviet Union, 1923–1939* (Ithaca, NY: Cornell University Press, 2001), https://doi.org/10.7591/9781501713323.

36   Kimberley A. Strassel, "Big Business's Sharp Left Turn," *Wall Street Journal,* January 14, 2021, https://www.wsj.com/articles/big-businesss-sharp-left-turn-11610665896.

37   Richard Hanania, "How Reagan Almost Crushed Wokeness," *Hanania Newsletter,* September 6, 2022, https://www.richardhanania.com/p/how-reagan-almost-crushed-wokeness.

38   Peter Baker, Lara Jakes, Julian E. Barnes, Sharon LaFraniere, and Edward Wong, "Trump's War on the 'Deep State' Turns Against Him," *New York Times,* October 23, 2019, https://www.nytimes.com/2019/10/23/us/politics/trump-deep-state-impeachment.html.

39   Brandon Barels, "It Took Conservatives 50 Years to Get a Reliable Majority on the Supreme Court. Here are 3 Reasons Why," *The Washington Post,* June 29, 2018, https://www.washingtonpost.com/news/monkey-cage/wp/2018/06/29/it-took-conservatives-50-years-to-get-a-reliable-majority-on-the-supreme-court-here-are-3-reasons-why/.

Chapter 3

40   Cass R. Sunstein, "Constitutionalism After the New Deal," *Harvard Law Review,* Vol. 101, No.2 (Dec., 1987), https://www.jstor.org/stable/1341264.

41   Richard A. Epstein, *How Progressives Rewrote the Constitution* (DC: Cato Institute, 2007).

42   John Yoo, "Franklin Roosevelt and Presidential Power," Chapman Law Review, 21 Article 10 (2018), https://digitalcommons.chapman.edu/cgi/viewcontent.cgi?article=1423&context=chapman-law-review.

43   Jer Clifton, "Many Differences Between Liberals and Conservatives May Boil Down to One Belief," *Scientific American,* March 1, 2023, https://www.scientificamerican.com/article/many-differences-between-liberals-and-conservatives-may-boil-down-to-one-belief/.

44   "Ronald Reagan's 1980 Neshoba County Fair Speech," *The Neshoba Democrat,* April 8, 2021, https://neshobademocrat.com/stories/ronald-reagans-1980-neshoba-county-fair-speech,49123.

45   U.S. Department of Labor, "Affirmative Action," accessed June 30, 2024, https://www.dol.gov/general/topic/hiring/affirmativeact#:~:text=For%20

federal%20contractors%20and%20subcontractors,efforts%2C%20 and%20other%20positive%20steps.

46 Fred Lucas, "Obama's Influence Could Continue After His Term Through His Political Appointees," *The Daily Signal,* August 3, 2016, https://www .dailysignal.com/2016/08/03/how-obamas-influence-could-continue-after -his-term-through-his-political-appointees/.

47 Kelsey Brugger, "EPA Revokes Trump-era 'Sue and Settle' Memo," *E&E News*, March 24, 2022, https://www.eenews.net/articles/ epa-revokes-trump-era-sue-and-settle-memo/.

48 Byron York, "When National Security Leaks Were Patriotic," *Washington Examiner,* April 11, 2023, https://www.washingtonexaminer.com/opinion/ when-national-security-leaks-were-patriotic.

49 U.S. Equal Employment Opportunity Commission, "Enforcement," accessed June 30, 2024, https://www.eeoc.gov/enforcement.

50 Trevor Barnes, "The Secret Cold War: The C.I.A. and American Foreign Policy in Europe, 1946-1956. Part I," *The Historical Journal*, Vol. 24, No. 2(Cambridge University Press, 1981), https://www.jstor.org/stable/2638793.

51 Yelena Dzhanova, "Intelligence Officials Withheld Sensitive Information from Trump While He Was in Office Because They Feared the "Damage' he Could Do if He Knew: Report,: *Business Insider,* August 14, 2022, https:// www.businessinsider.com/intelligence-officials-purposely-withheld-info -from-former-president-trump-report-2022-8,

52 Thomas A. Hemphill, "The Administrative Threat," *Cato Institute*, Fall 2017, https://www.cato.org/regulation/fall-2017/administrative-threat.

53 David Ignatius, "Why Did Obama Dawdle on Russia's Hacking?," *The Washington Post*, January 12, 2017, https://www. washingtonpost.com/opinions/why-did-obama-dawdle-on-russias -hacking/2017/01/12/75f878a0-d90c-11e6-9a36-1d296534b31e_story.html.

54 Adam Goldman and Michael S. Schmidt, "Rod Rosenstein Suggested Secretly Recording Trump and Discussed 25th Amendment," *New York Times*, September 21, 2018, https://www.nytimes.com/2018/09/21/us/ politics/rod-rosenstein-wear-wire-25th-amendment.html#:~:text=with%20 the%20discussion.-,Mr.,replied%20animatedly%20that%20he%20was.

55 William Barr, "Attorney General William P. Barr Delivers the 19th Annual Barbara K. Olson Memorial Lecture at the Federalist Society's 2019 National Lawyers Convention," (speech, Washington, D.C., 2019), U.S. Department of Justice Office of Public Affairs, https://www.justice.gov/ opa/speech/attorney-general-william-p-barr-delivers-19th-annual-barbara -k-olson-memorial-lecture.

56 Stephen F. Cohen, "Russiagate or Intelgate?" *The Nation*, February 7, 2018, https://www.thenation.com/article/archive/russiagate-or-intelgate/.

57 Toni Monkovic, "50 Years of Electoral College Maps: How the U.S. Turned Red and Blue," *New York Times*, August 22, 2016, https://www.nytimes.com/2016/08/23/upshot/50-years-of-electoral-college-maps-how-the-us-turned-red-and-blue.html.

58 Monkovic, *Electoral College Maps: Red and Blue.*

59 Kenan Malik, "Politics of Disillusionment and the Rise of Trump," *Aljazeera*, March 6, 2016, https://www.aljazeera.com/opinions/2016/3/6/politics-of-disillusionment-and-the-rise-of-trump.

60 Lou Cannon, "Ronald Reagan: Domestic Affairs," *University of Virginia Miller Center*, accessed June 30, 2024, https://millercenter.org/president/reagan/domestic-affairs.

61 "Education Dept. Won't Be Abolished: Reagan Backs Down, Citing Little Support for Killing Agency," *Los Angeles Times*, January 29, 1985, https://www.latimes.com/archives/la-xpm-1985-01-29-mn-13948-story.html.

62 White House, "President Trump's Coronavirus Response Has Saved Over 2 Million Lives and Outperformed Other Nations," (Washington, D.C., October 27, 2020), https://trumpwhitehouse.archives.gov/briefings-statements/president-trumps-coronavirus-response-saved-2-million-lives-outperformed-nations/.

63 Jamie Raskin, "Reps. Raskin, Chu Lead Colleagues in Introduction of Bill to Award Congressional Gold Medal to Americans Who Rescued Holocaust Refugees," news releases, April 18, 2023, https://raskin.house.gov/2023/4/reps-raskin-chu-lead-colleagues-in-introduction-of-bill-to-award-congressional-gold-medal-to-americans-who-rescued-holocaust-refugees.

64 Federalist Society, "What Should Congress do?" *Article I Initiative*, accessed June 24, 2024, https://fedsoc.org/divisions/article-i-initiative.

65 National Immigration Law Center, "Supreme Court Overturns Trump Administration's Termination of DACA," press release, June 22, 2020, https://www.nilc.org/issues/daca/alert-supreme-court-overturns-trump-administrations-termination-of-daca/.

Chapter 4

66 David Bernhardt, *You Report to Me*, (Encounter Books, 2023).

67 "Executive Order 13957 of October 21, 2020, on Creating Schedule F in the Excepted Service," *Code of Federal Regulations*, title 5 (2020). https://trumpwhitehouse.archives.gov/presidential-actions/executive-order-creating-schedule-f-excepted-service/.

68 EO 13957, Schedule F.

69 Donald Moynihan, "Trump Got Burned by a Major Mistake in His Frist Term. He Won't Make It Again." *Slate*, July 27, 2022, https://slate.com/news-and-politics/2022/07/donald-trump-schedule-f-civil-service-authoritarian.html.

70 Robin Bravender, "The Name is Beale. John Beale." *Greenwire*, October 28, 2013, http://www.eenews.net/stories/1059989515.

71 Michael J. Gaynor, "The Suit Who Spooked the EPA," *Washingtonian*, March 4, 2014, http://www.washingtonian.com/articles/people/the-suit-who-spooked-the-epa/.

72 Gaynor, *The Suit*.

73 Erich Wagner, "OPM Will End Agencies' Maximum Telework Status Next Month," *Government Executive*, April 19, 2023, https://www.govexec.com/workforce/2023/04/opm-will-end-agencies-maximum-telework-status-next-month/385387/.

74 *Government Employee Fair Treatment Act of 2019*, Public Law 116-1 (2019), https://www.congress.gov/116/plaws/publ1/PLAW-116publ1.pdf.

75 Lucian McMahon, "EPA Porn Enthusiast Still Employed at EPA," *Reason*, September 9, 2014, https://reason.com/2014/09/24/epa-porn-enthusiast-still-employed/.

76 McMahon, *EPA Porn Enthusiast Still Employed*.

77 Erin Peterson, "Presidential Power Surges," *Harvard Law Today*, July 17, 2019, https://hls.harvard.edu/today/presidential-power-surges/.

78 "Executive Order 11478 of August 8, 1969, on Equal Employment Opportunity in the Federal Government," *Code of Federal Regulations*, title 3 (1969). https://www.archives.gov/federal-register/codification/executive-order/11478.html

79 "Executive Order 11246, As Amended of August 8, 1969, on Equal Employment Opportunity," *Code of Federal Regulations*, title 3 (1969). https://www.dol.gov/agencies/ofccp/executive-order-11246/as-amended

80 Regents of the University of California v. Bakke, 438 US 265 (1978).

81 Ruth Igielnik, "A Majority of Americans Say Race Should Not be a Factor in College Adminissions," *New York Times*, June 29, 2023, https://www.nytimes.com/2023/06/29/us/politics/affirmative-action-polls.html.

82 Richard Hanania, "Speech to the Yale Federalist Society," *Hanania Newsletter*, May 23, 2023, https://www.richardhanania.com/p/speech-to-the-yale-federalist-society.

83 Mike Lillis and Mychael Schnell, "Affirmative Action Ruling Sharply Divides Demis, GOP," *The Hill*, June 29, 2023, https://thehill.com/homenews/house/4073932-affirmative-action-ruling-sharply-divides-dems-gop/.

84   Christopher F. Rufo, *America's Cultural Revolution*, (Broadside Books, 2023).

Chapter 5

85   Andrew Prokop, "The Hidden Politics of New York City's New Ranked-choice Voting System," *Vox*, June 16, 2021, https://www.vox.com/22443775/ranked-choice-voting-explained-new-york-strategy.

86   Katie Glueck, "Evangelicals Still Peeved over Pence's Religious Freedom Act Flip," *Politico*, July 15, 2016, https://www.politico.com/story/2016/07/trump-vp-pick-mike-pence-evangelicals-225623.

87   Ryan King, "Dumb People Always Overpay for These 21 Things," *Washington Examiner*, May 30, 2023, https://www.washingtonexaminer.com/news/campaigns/mike-pence-blasts-debt-limit-deal.

88   Zachary B. Wolf, "24 Former Trump Allies and Aides Who Turned Against Him," *CNN*, October 3, 2023, https://www.cnn.com/2023/10/03/politics/donald-trump-former-allies-what-matters/index.html.

89   Chris Menahan, "Pompeo Hire 'Never Trumper' Mary Kissel as a Top Adviser to State Department," *Information Liberation*, November 28, 2018, https://www.informationliberation.com/?id=59446.

90   *An Act to prescribe penalties for certain acts of violence or intimidation, and for other purposes*, HR 2516, 90th Cong., 2nd sess., *Congressional Record* 9620 (April 10, 1968), https://www.govinfo.gov/content/pkg/GPO-CRECB-1968-pt8/pdf/GPO-CRECB-1968-pt8-1-2.pdf.

91   Jacob Heilbrunn, "George H. W. Bush, the Last Great Liberal Republican," *The Spectator*, December 1, 2018, https://www.spectator.co.uk/article/george-h-w-bush-the-last-great-liberal-republican/.

92   Bianca Seward and Sarah Dean, "Mike Pence Grilled on His Support for Ukraine by Tucker Carlson," *NBC News*, July 14, 2023, https://www.nbcnews.com/meet-the-press/meetthepressblog/mike-pence-grilled-support-ukraine-tucker-carlson-rcna94321.

93   Brian Domitrovic, "George H. W. Bush's Voodoo Rhetoric," *Forbes*, December 2, 2018, https://www.forbes.com/sites/briandomitrovic/2018/12/02/george-h-w-bushs-voodoo-rhetoric/?sh=468a944e798a.

94   Lou Cannon, "Ronald Reagan: Campaigns and Elections," *University of Virginia Miller Center*, accessed June 30, 2024, https://millercenter.org/president/reagan/campaigns-and-elections.

95   Cannon, *Ronald Reagan*.

96   Silvio Simonetti, "Getting the Reagan Revolution Right," *Acton Institute*, May 23, 2019, https://rlo.acton.org/archives/108875-the-reagan-revolution-demystified.html.

97   United States Department of Education Office of Civil Rights, *Dear Colleague*, Candice Jackson, September 22, 2017, https://www2.ed.gov/about/offices/list/ocr/letters/colleague-title-ix-201709.pdf.

98   James Baker, "The Man Who Ran Washington: James Baker," interview by David Marchick, *Blog*, Center for Presidential Transition, June 29, 2020, https://presidentialtransition.org/blog/the-man-who-ran-washington-james-baker/.

99   Carla Hall, "The Amazing Endowment Scramble," *The Washington Post*, December 13, 1981, https://www.washingtonpost.com/archive/lifestyle/style/1981/12/13/the-amazing-endowment-scramble/b16738d2-5d6b-4260-aeda-a7e435c455e9/.

100 The National Endowment for the Humanities, "Grants," accessed July 1, 2024, https://www.neh.gov/grants.

101 Arthur Meier Schlesinger, *The Disuniting of America: Reflection on a Multicultural Society* (W.W. Norton & Company, 1998).

102 National Endowment for the Humanities, "To Reclaim a Legacy: A Report on the Humanities in Higher Education," William J. Bennett. ED 247880, Washington, D.C.: 1984. Accessed July 1, 2024, https://eric.ed.gov/?id=ED247880.

103 Tim Nelson, "The Trump Administration's Highly Politicized Roll Back of Obama-Era Fair Housing Rule Raises Concerns," *Architectural Digest*, July 30, 2020, https://www.architecturaldigest.com/story/trump-hud-fair-housing-act.

104 Michael Levenson, "As They Head to Harvard Gary Cohn and Heidi Heitkamp Criticize Shutdown," *The Boston Globe*, January 17, 2019, https://www.bostonglobe.com/metro/2019/01/17/they-head-harvard-gary-cohn-and-heidi-heitkamp-criticize-shutdown/nDoJbmWksuJf9Qoj8LiTbI/story.html.

105 Howard Gleckman, "Trump's Zero-Sum Choice: A Wall or A Tax Cut," *Forbes*, August 23, 2017, https://www.forbes.com/sites/beltway/2017/08/23/trumps-zero-sum-choice-a-wall-or-a-tax-cut/?sh=5ce25f95382c.

106 Brakkton Booker, "DeSantis Takes Aim at Trump's Signature Criminal Justice Reform Law, *Politico*, June 18, 2023, https://www.politico.com/news/2023/06/18/desantis-trump-criminal-justice-reform-00102516.

107 Dustin Jones and Devin Speak, "Trump Wants the Death Penalty for Drug Dealers. Here's Why that Probably Won't Happen," *NPR*, May 10 2023, https://www.npr.org/2023/05/10/1152847242/trump-campaign-execute-drug-dealers-smugglers-traffickers-death-row#:~:text=Hip%2DHop%20 50-,Trump's%202024%20campaign%20promise%20to%20execute%20 drug%20offenders%20is%20a,for%20drug%20dealers%20and%20 smugglers.

108 Julian E. Barnes and Helene Cooper, "Trump Discussed Pulling U.S. From NATO, Aides Say Amid New Concerns Over Russia, *New York Times*, January 14, 2019, https://www.nytimes.com/2019/01/14/us/politics/nato-president-trump.html.

109 Executive Order 13950 of September 22, 2020, on Combating Race and Sex Stereotyping," *Code of Federal Regulations*, title 40 (2020), https://trumpwhitehouse.archives.gov/presidential-actions/executive-order-combating-race-sex-stereotyping/.

110 "About Us," American Moment, accessed July 1, 2024, https://www.americanmoment.org/about/.

Chapter 6

111 National School Choice Week, "2023-2024 Trends," June 14, 2024, https://schoolchoiceweek.com/trends/.

112 Katie J.M. Baker, "Republicans Doing Pretty Great Job of Shutting Down Abortion Clinics," *Jezebel*, August 26, 2013, https://jezebel.com/republicans-doing-pretty-great-job-of-shutting-down-abo-1201159600.

113 David Cole, "Kennedy's Legacy: A Moderating Force and a Concern for Equal Dignity," *ACLU*, June 28, 2018, https://www.aclu.org/news/reproductive-freedom/kennedys-legacy-moderating-force-and-concern-equal-dignity.

114 James R. Belpedio, "Felix Frankfurter," *Free Speech Center at Middle Tennessee State University*, August 7, 2023, https://www.mtsu.edu/first-amendment/article/1330/felix-frankfurter.

115 Chris Schmidt, "The Forgotten Backlash Against the Warren Court," *IIT Chicago-Kent College of Law SCOTUS Now,* December 30, 2014, https://blogs.kentlaw.iit.edu/iscotus/forgotten-backlash-warren-court/.

116 "Roe v. Wade," *Oyez*, Accessed July 1, 2024, https://www.oyez.org/cases/1971/70-18.

117 "George Wallace: Settin' the Woods on Fire, 1968 Campaign," American Experience *PBS*, April 23, 2000, https://www.pbs.org/wgbh/americanexperience/features/wallace-1968-campaign/.

118 Steven Pinker, "Decivilization in the 1960s," *Human Figurations* 2, no. 2 (July 2013), https://quod.lib.umich.edu/h/humfig/11217607.0002.206/--decivilization-in-the-1960s?rgn=main;view=fulltext.

119 "John Paul Stevens," *Oyez*, accessed July 1, 2024, https://www.oyez.org/justices/john_paul_stevens.

120 Martin Pengelly, "Key Democrat attacks US Supreme Court Chief Justice over Ethics Scandal," *The Guardian,* July 7, 2023, https://www.theguardian.com/us-news/2023/jul/07/us-supreme-court-john-roberts-dick-durbin.

121 Lou Cannon, "Ronald Reagan: Campaigns and Elections," *UVA: Miller Center,* April 2017, https://millercenter.org/president/reagan/campaigns-and-elections.

122 Philip Wegmann, "Amid foreign agent drama, memo reveals $20M to Hunter and Biden family," *The Highland County Press,* August 11, 2023, https://highlandcountypress.com/amid-foreign-agent-drama-memo-reveals-20m-hunter-and-biden-family#gsc.tab=0.

123 Stanford Encyclopedia of Philosophy, "Prisoner's Dilemma", *Stanford Encyclopedia of Philosophy,* (April 2, 2019), https://plato.stanford.edu/entries/prisoner-dilemma/.

124 Michael Anton, "What Progressives Did to Cities", *First Things,* December 20, 2021, https://www.firstthings.com/web-exclusives/2021/12/what-progressives-did-to-cities.

125 Steven Johnson, 'The 15 Richest Countries in the U.S.", *U.S. News,* December 20, 2023, https://www.usnews.com/news/healthiest-communities/slideshows/richest-counties-in-america.

126 Office of Fossil Energy and Carbon Management, "Department of Energy Releases Report on Economic and National Security Impacts of a Hydraulic Fracturing Ban," *Energy.gov,* January 14, 2021, https://www.energy.gov/fecm/articles/department-energy-releases-report-economic-and-national-security-impacts-hydraulic.

127 Office of Fossil Energy and Carbon Management, "Department of Energy Releases Report on Economic and National Security Impacts of a Hydraulic Fracturing Ban," *Energy.gov,* January 14, 2021, https://www.energy.gov/fecm/articles/department-energy-releases-report-economic-and-national-security-impacts-hydraulic.

128 Dorthy Neufeld, "Mapped: Global Energy Prices, by Country in 2022," *Visual Capitalist,* December 3, 2022, https://www.visualcapitalist.com/mapped-global-energy-prices-by-country-in-2022/.

129 Huntington, Samuel, *The Soldier and the State* (Harvard University Press: Cambridge, MA, 1981), https://www.hup.harvard.edu/catalog.php?isbn=9780674817364.

130 Victor Davis Hanson, "Not-So-Retiring Retired Military Leaders," *National Review,* June 7, 2020, https://www.nationalreview.com/2020/06/not-so-retiring-retired-military-leaders/.

131 Victor Davis Hanson, "VICTOR DAVIS HANSON: There's a problem in the upper reaches of our military," *Las Vegas Review-Journal,* September 4, 2021, https://www.reviewjournal.com/opinion/opinion-columns/victor-davis-hanson/victor-davis-hanson-theres-a-problem-in-the-upper-reaches-of-our-military-2434016/.

132 James Rosen, "Nixon and the Chiefs," *The Atlantic*, April 2002, https://www.theatlantic.com/magazine/archive/2002/04/nixon-and-the-chiefs/302473/.

133 Lolita Baldor and Robert Burns, "WATCH: Gen. Milley explains his calls with China over concerns about President Trump," *PBS News*, September 28, 2021, https://www.pbs.org/newshour/politics/watch-gen-milley-explains-his-calls-with-china-over-concerns-about-president-trump.

Chapter 7

134 Emily Brooks, "The Hill's Changemakers: Kevin Roberts, president of the Heritage Foundation," *The Hill*, December 13, 2023, https://thehill.com/changemakers/4346310-the-hills-changemakers-kevin-roberts-president-of-the-heritage-foundation/.

135 Spencer Chretien, "Project 2025," *The Heritage Foundation*, January 31, 2023, https://www.heritage.org/conservatism/commentary/project-2025?gclid=CjoKCQjwrfymBhCTARIsADXTabmhzncz_vegeCc4N5JUTbLJ8nMmfNT8jyqBYfBjpSwZGmUKn2YKbMYaAiHWEALw_wcB.

136 Allan Smith, "Vivek Ramaswamy wants to trigger mass layoffs at federal agencies—and he thinks the Supreme Court will back him up," *NBC News*, September 12, 2023, https://www.nbcnews.com/politics/2024-election/vivek-ramaswamy-wants-trigger-mass-layoffs-federal-agencies-thinks-sco-rcna104676.

137 Lucy Madison," Romney on immigration: I'm for "self-deportation," *Politics*, January 24, 2012, https://www.cbsnews.com/news/romney-on-immigration-im-for-self-deportation/.

138 Mike Wendling, "Why is Republican candidate Vivek Ramaswamy doubling down on conspiracy theories?" *BBC*, December 15, 2023, https://www.bbc.com/news/world-us-canada-67655552.

139 Lauren Sforza, "Ramaswamy says at debate he would end birthright citizenship, echoing Trump," *The Hill*, September 28, 2023, https://thehill.com/homenews/campaign/4227711-ramaswamy-end-birthright-citizenship-2024-debate/.

140 Matt Berg, "DeSantis backs Tuberville on military holds, denounces Pentagon abortion policy," *Politico*, July 20, 2023, https://www.politico.com/news/2023/07/20/tuberville-military-desantis-abortion-00107289.

141 Cheryl Teh, "Chris Christie says the DOJ likely had 'no choice' but to raid Mar-a-Lago, *Business Insider*, September 12, 2024, https://www.businessinsider.com/chris-christie-trump-doj-no-choice-raid-mar-a-lago-2022-9?utm_source=reddit.com.

142 Business Today Desk, "'Why has Dept of Defense never passed an audit?':
Vivek Ramaswamy's latest salvo against US federal system," *Business
Today,* November 4, 2023, https://www.businesstoday.in/latest/world/
story/why-has-dept-of-defense-never-passed-an-audit-vivek-ramaswamys
-latest-salvo-against-us-federal-system-404601-2023-11-04.

143 Fox & Friends, "Trump Issues Warning: U.S. 'can't have a woke military',"
June 3, 2024, https://www.foxnews.com/video/6354209640112.

144 U.S. Senate Committee on Appropriations, *Bill Summary: Defense Fiscal
Year 2024 Appropriations Bill,* (Washington, D.C., 2024), https://www
.appropriations.senate.gov/imo/media/doc/fy24_defense_bill_summary
.pdf.

145 ZipRecruiter Writers, "Federal Government Salary in Washington,
D.C.," *ZipRecruiter,* https://www.ziprecruiter.com/Salaries/
Federal-Government-Salary-in-Washington,D.C..

146 USA Facts Writers, "Three charts on diversity in the federal government's
workforce," *USAFacts,* March 28, 2023, https://usafacts.org/articles/
three-charts-on-diversity-in-the-federal-governments-workforce/.

147 United States Government Accountability Office, "FEDERAL REAL
PROPERTY: Agencies Need New Benchmarks to Measure and Shed
Underutilized Space," *Report to Congressional Committees,* (October 2023),
https://www.gao.gov/products/gao-24-107006#:~:text=Seventeen%20
of%20the%2024%20federal,February%2C%20and%20March%20
of%202023.

148 Sen. Todd Young, "Viewpoint: Indiana senator: IRS customer service
has hit an all-time low," *South Bend Tribune,* March 23, 2022, https://
www.southbendtribune.com/story/opinion/columns/2022/03/23/
customer-service-irs-has-been-abysmal-recent-years/9454565002/.

149 Michael Gibbs, Friederike Mengel, and Christoph Siemroth, July 2021,
"Work from Home and Productivity: Evidence from Personnel and
Analytics Data on IT professionals," Working Paper no. 2021-56, *Becker
Friedman Institute,* Chicago, IL, https://bfi.uchicago.edu/wp-content/
uploads/2021/05/BFI_WP_2021-56.pdf.

150 Mike Dorning, "Washington Suffers as Federal Employees Work From
Home," *Bloomberg,* March 9, 2023, https://www.bloomberg.com/news/
features/2023-03-09/wfh-federal-employees-have-republicans-some-dems
-demanding-return-to-office.

Chapter 8

151 James Oliphant and Gram Slattery, "Trump's second-term agenda:
deportations, trade wars, NATO rethink," *Reuters,* June 18, 2024, https://

www.reuters.com/world/us/payback-time-trump-plans-mass-firings
-deportations-second-term-2023-11-14/.

152 Steven Nelson, "Lock Him up? Lawmakers Renew Calls for James Clapper Perjury Charges," *U.S. News,* November 17, 2016, https://www.usnews.com/news/articles/2016-11-17/lawmakers-resume-calls-for-james-clapper-perjury-charges.

153 Russell Berman, "The Open Plot to Dismantle the Federal Government," *The Atlantic,* September 24, 2023, https://www.theatlantic.com/politics/archive/2023/09/trump-desantis-republicans-dismantle-deep-state/675378/.

154 Victor Davis Hanson, "VICTOR DAVIS HANSON: There's a problem in the upper reaches of our military," *Las Vegas Review-Journal,* September 4, 2021, https://www.reviewjournal.com/opinion/opinion-columns/victor-davis-hanson/victor-davis-hanson-theres-a-problem-in-the-upper-reaches-of-our-military-2434016/.

155 Kristen Holmes, "Trump's Radical second-term agenda would wield executive power in unprecedented ways," *CNN,* November 16, 2023, https://www.cnn.com/2023/11/16/politics/trump-agenda-second-term/index.html.

156 Hugh Hewitt, "Former President Donald Trump On President Biden, Support for Israel, The War In Ukraine, Campaign 2024, and What a Second Trump Term Would Look Like," *HughHewitt Podcast,* July 1, 2024, https://hughhewitt.com/former-president-donald-trump-on-president-biden-support-for-israel-the-war-in-ukraine-campaign-2024-and-what-a-second-trump-term-would-look-like.

157 Jon Schweppe, "Why Did Corporations Go 'Woke?' It's Not About the Free Market," *Newsweek,* August 18, 2023, https://www.newsweek.com/why-did-corporations-go-woke-its-not-about-free-market-opinion-1820373.

158 Lawrence Richard, "Vivek Ramaswamy says he'll repeal affirmative action 'without apology' on day 1 if elected president," *Fox News,* February 22, 2023, https://www.foxnews.com/politics/vivek-ramaswamy-repeal-affirmative-action-without-apology-day-1-elected-president.

159 Tim Hains, "Ramaswamy: LGBTQIA+ Movement Has Become A Cult, "A New Culture Of Oppression," *RealClear Politics,* May 2, 2023, https://www.realclearpolitics.com/video/2023/05/02/ramaswamy_lgbtqia_movement_has_become_a_cult.html.

160 Tom Shoop, "Meet the long-shot presidential candidate who wants term limits for federal employees," *Workforce,* June 27, 2023, https://web.archive.org/web/20230627173714/https://www.govexec.com/workforce/2023/06/meet-long-shot-presidential-candidate-who-wants-term-limits-federal-employees/387960/.

161 Alexi McCammond, "The Next Trump: Younger and to the Right," *Axios*, May 12, 2023, https://web.archive.org/web/20230627173715/https://www .axios.com/2023/05/12/vivek-ramaswamy-trump-gop-2024.

162 Business Today Desk, "'Why has Dept of Defense never passed an audit?': Vivek Ramaswamy's latest salvo against US federal system," *Business Today*, November 4, 2023, https://www.businesstoday.in/latest/world/ story/why-has-dept-of-defense-never-passed-an-audit-vivek-ramaswamys -latest-salvo-against-us-federal-system-404601-2023-11-04/.

163 Gregory Krieg and Eric Bradner, "Takeaways from CNN's Town Hall with Nikki Haley," *CNN*, June 4, 2023, https://www.rferl.org/a/us-nikki-haley -ukraine-support-2024-election/32445633.html.

164 Gareth Evans, "Vivek Ramaswamy: Eight Things Republican Presidential Candidate Believes," *BBC*, September 28, 2023, https://www.bbc.com/ news/world-us-canada-66603166.

165 Russia Matters Staff and Associates, "Kissinger on Russia: Insights and Recommendations," *Russia Matters*, December 1, 2023, https://www.russiamatters.org/analysis/ kissinger-russia-insights-and-recommendations.

166 Readers, "Vivek Ramaswamy's Plan to Defend Tiawan," *Wall Street Journal*, August 28, 2023, https://www.wsj.com/articles/vivek-ramaswamy -plan-to-defend-taiwan-arm-semiconductors-debate-5d5f751d.

167 Leslie Postal, "Florida board votes to ban critical race theory from state classrooms," *Orlando Sentinel*, June 10, 2021, https://www .orlandosentinel.com/news/education/os-ne-critical-race-state-board -20210610-7pzv23n7rjeixi3a4veffugalq-story.html.

168 Jocelyn Gecker, "How Ron DeSantis used Florida schools to become a culture warrior," *Associated Press*, August 23, 2023, https://apnews.com/article/ron-desantis-education-gop-debate -723e18d19912b97696f3ad2c9d77e099#:~:text=A%20major%20 theme%20of%20DeSantis,on%20racial%20and%20gender%20biases.

169 Alex Oliveira, "Shocking 3.8 million migrants have entered US since Biden took office – 1.5 million sneaked in and are still here," *New York Post*, September 21, 2023, https://nypost.com/2023/09/21/ shocking-3-8-million-migrants-have-entered-us-since-biden-took-office/.

170 Julia Mueller, "Biden approval on immigration drops 8 points since last month: poll," *The Hill*, December 18, 2023, https://thehill.com/homenews/ administration/4366570-biden-approval-on-immigration-drops-8-points -since-last-month-poll/.

171 Bernd Debusmann Jr., "Why are migrants in the U.S. being sent to Democrat-run areas?," *BBC*, September 16, 2022, https://www.bbc.com/ news/world-us-canada-62921858.

172 Nicole Narea, "How Florida became the Center of the Republican Universe," *Vox*, September 18, 2023, https://www.vox.com/politics/23848897/florida-red-trump-desantis-republican-2024-election#:~:text=Florida%20is%20now%20a%20Republican,migration%20and%20has%20for%20years.

173 Hailey Branson-Potts, "California vs. Florida why are People moving from One State to the Other?," *L.A. Times,* November 29th, 2023, https://www.latimes.com/california/story/2023-11-29/california-vs-florida-why-are-people-moving-from-one-state-to-the-other#:~:text=Last%20year%2C%20according%20to%20newly,growing%20state%20of%2022%20million.

Chapter 9

174 Alan Feuer, "In Harsh Rebuke, Appeals Court Rejects Trump's Election Challenge in Pennsylvania," *New York Times,* November 27, 2020, https://www.nytimes.com/2020/11/27/us/politics/trump-pennsylvania-appeals-court.html.

175 Donald J. Trump for President, Inc. v. Secretary Commonwealth of Pennsylvania et al., No. 20-3371, slip op. (3d Cir. Nov. 27, 2020), https://www2.ca3.uscourts.gov/opinarch/203371np.pdf.

176 Kevin Johnson, "William Barr: Democrats' investigations into Trump are Political Harassment meant to 'sabotage' his Presidency," *USA Today,* November 15, 2019, https://www.usatoday.com/story/news/politics/2019/11/15/barr-trumps-political-opponents-seeking-sabotage-administration/4201431002/.

177 Jan Wolfe and Ismail Shakil, "U.S. Settles with Black Live Matter Protesters violently cleared from White House Park," *Reuters,* April 13, 2022, https://www.reuters.com/world/us/us-justice-dept-settles-cases-related-police-response-dc-anti-racism-protests-2022-04-13/.

178 Luke Mullins and Patrick Hruby, "The Caps and Wizards Are Leaving D.C.: Who's to Blame?," *Washingtonian,* December 21, 2023, https://www.washingtonian.com/2023/12/21/the-caps-and-wizards-are-leaving-dc-whos-to-blame/#:~:text=Last%20week%2C%20Ted%20Leonsis%20shocked,new%20stadium%20in%20Potomac%20Yard.

179 Christian Greer, "America's Mayors Should Take Marion Barry as a Model. Seriously.," *The Nation,* February 14, 2022, https://www.thenation.com/article/politics/marion-barry-washington-mayor/.

180 Daniel Larison, "Biden's 2023 Foreign Policy was a Bust," *Responsible Statecraft,* December 26, 2023, https://responsiblestatecraft.org/biden-foreign-policy-2023/.

181 Lolita Baldor and Tara Copp, "Defense Secretary Lloyd Austin released from hospital after complications from prostate cancer surgery he kept secret," *PBS News*, January 15, 2024, https://www.pbs.org/newshour/nation/defense-secretary-lloyd-austin-released-from-hospital-after-complications-from-prostate-cancer-surgery-he-kept-secret.

182 Revolver News, "Declassified Military Report Exposes hidden Links Between Wokeness and the American Regime," *Revolver News*, June 30, 2022, https://revolver.news/2021/11/declassified-military-report-exposes-hidden-links-between-wokeness-and-the-regime/.

183 Walter Mead, "Scolding isn't a Foreign Policy," *The Wall Street Journal*, April 17, 2023, https://www.wsj.com/articles/scolding-isnt-a-foreign-policy-blinken-philippines-china-vietnam-communism-pragmatism-morality-3028f9c.